REA

ALLEN COUNTY PUBLIC LIBRARY
ACPL ITEM
3 1833 02174 3254

DISCARDED

B V2
Mar
Two of a kind

S0-CBH-093

DO NOT REMOVE
CARDS FROM POCKET

ALLEN COUNTY PUBLIC LIBRARY

FORT WAYNE, INDIANA 46802

You may return this book to any agency, branch,
or bookmobile of the Allen County Public Library.

DEMCO

Two of a Kind

The Tom and Dick Van Arsdale Story

by

Kerry D. Marshall

Scott Publications

Indianapolis, Indiana

Scott Publications
First Trade Edition   October 1992

Copyright @ August 1992 by Kerry D. Marshall

All rights reserved.   No part of this book may be
reproduced or transmitted in any form or by any means,
electronic   or   mechanical,   including   photocopying,
recording, or by any information storage and retrieval
system, without the permission of the publisher, except
where permitted by law.

Allen County Public Library
900 Webster Street
PO Box 2270
Fort Wayne, IN 46801-2270

Library of Congress Catalog Number: 92-061487

ISBN 0-9630362-2-X

Other Books by Mr. Marshall include:

A Boy, A Ball, and a Dream: The Marvin Wood Story
(ISBN 0-9630362-0-3)

and

The Jackie Robinson of High School Basketball

This Book was manufactured in the United States of America.

Acknowledgements

The creation of this book would not have been possible without the help of many people. I am especially grateful for the assistance of my editor, Sherilyn Creutz, the fine people at Lebco, Inc. who handled the typesetting, John Lyon and Creative Color, Inc. for their quality camera work, Greg Thompson and Miles Press for the printing, and H & H Bookbinders for wrapping it all up.

I also extend my gratitude to all of the individuals who willingly took the time to talk to me about Dick and Tom Van Arsdale.

Thanks to my wife, Rebecca, who makes so many things possible.

To

Hilda, Barbara, Kathy,

Jason, Jill, Kerrie,

Chris, and Amy.

Introduction

In 1970, I left Kansas State to become the head coach of the Phoenix Suns. I had been coaching for many years, but the job with Phoenix would be my first in the NBA. I didn't know quite what to expect, but I was anxious to get to Phoenix and find out.

When I arrived in town, one of the first people I met was Dick Van Arsdale. Dick was the Suns' team captain and I was immediately impressed with him. Little did I know that was the beginning of a friendship that would last for years.

When I saw what he could do on a basketball court, I couldn't wait for the season to begin. Dick was a fierce competitor. He approached every practice and every game with the same philosophy---give one hundred percent. He led our team, not with fiery speeches or displays of emotion, but with hustle and a work ethic that was hard to match.

Several years down the road, while coaching in Atlanta, I was asked for my input on a possible deal for Tom Van Arsdale. Knowing that he and his brother were as similar in their basketball skills as they were in appearance, my advice was that we do anything we could to get him. Tom played for me for two years and brought to the court the same desire and intensity I had seen in his brother. On and off the basketball court, Dick and Tom were a class act.

The attitudes these two young men displayed are a tribute to fine parental guidance and excellent teaching and coaching. Born and raised in Greenwood, Indiana by devoted parents, Dick and Tom have made the most of a background that emphasized respect, hard work, and basketball. As I've grown to know them over the years, I've had the privilege of meeting their mother, Hilda, and I didn't have to be around her long to understand why her boys have become what they are. She and her husband, Raymond, gave them a great foundation from which to build their lives.

While Dick and Tom are excellent examples of what dedication, hard work, and self confidence can bring, I stop short of recommending them or any other professional athlete as a role model. A role model represents an image of something that is close to being perfect. Professional athletes, even fine examples such as Dick and Tom, are far from perfect. I could never recommend that anyone pattern their life after someone else's life. However, I do believe that we can examine other people and learn from their experiences to improve our own lives. In that regard, I believe that Dick and Tom are two fine <u>examples</u> for young people and adults to examine. They exemplify much of what is good both in professional sports and in our society.

As the years have passed and the twins have turned from the basketball court to other careers, they remain two of my best friends. And, while I know them as two entirely different individuals, when I look at what they have achieved and how they have gone about it. I realize that they are indeed---Two of a Kind.

Table of Contents

"These things I have spoken to you, that in me you may have peace. In the world you will have tribulation; but be of good cheer, I have overcome the world."

John 16:33

Chapter 1

Raymond "Van" Van Arsdale holds his twin sons.

Basketball, invented in 1891 by Dr. James Naismith, found its way west into Indiana and soon became a part of the state's culture. From the Franklin "Wonder Five" of the early twenties to the "Milan Miracle" of 1954, and on up to Robert Knight's amazing tenure at Indiana University, "Hoosier Hysteria" has produced some of basketball's brightest stars and memorable legends.

Only a few of the thousands of young men and women who annually compete in Indiana high school basketball become stars. Those who do are the role models for the next generation of young Hoosiers, who practice their craft in driveways and playgrounds while dreaming of creating their own piece of basketball history.

Among the many role models Indiana basketball has produced, perhaps two of the finest have been Dick and Tom Van Arsdale. Tom and Dick, identical twins, excelled in basketball at Indianapolis Manual High School, Indiana University, and later starred in the NBA. Throughout their careers both have demonstrated the traits basketball fans admire in their heros. Dick and Tom were consummate team players. They tried to give one hundred percent every time they were on the court, and always demonstrated a fierce desire to win. They displayed humility in victory and good sportsmanship in defeat. Away from basketball, the twins have demonstrated the same qualities that made them excellent role models on the court.

In an age where many sports heros are more admired for the greatness of their athletic ability rather than the depth of their character, the Van Arsdale twins remind us that it is possible to be both a great athlete and a good person.

* *

The twins attribute much of their success to the values

instilled by their parents, Hilda and Raymond "Van" Van Arsdale. Raised in Greenwood, Indiana, a suburb of Indianapolis, Tom and Dick were brought up to believe that they could do anything they wanted to do and be anything they wanted to be---provided they were willing to work hard and maintain a positive attitude.

Their father, whom almost everyone refers to as "Van," taught school and coached track at Manual High School. He had graduated from Wabash College where he excelled in track, specializing in the broad jump. His longest jump, twenty-three feet six inches, has been a Wabash College record for over sixty years. In fact, if not for an untimely thigh injury, Van might have been a member of the United States Olympic team.

While teaching at Manual, Van met Hilda Thomas through a mutual friend. They married in October 1940 and three years later the twins were born. Hilda remembers the birth of her only children as if it happened only yesterday, especially since she had no idea she was carrying twins. "I started into heavy labor on a Saturday about seven weeks before the baby was actually due. The labor pains continued all through Saturday and on into Sunday morning, when Van took me to the hospital. By Sunday night, the pains were not as bad or as frequent, but the doctor said that if I didn't progress any more by the morning that he'd have to do a cesarean section. He thought there wasn't any way to save the baby from being born premature without risking my life.

"As it turned out, my labor pains returned and the twins were born early the next morning. The doctor had given me a little anesthesia to help with the pain so I wasn't awake when Tom was born. When I came to I heard someone saying that they needed another incubator because there might be another one.

"Discovering that I'd had twins left me flabbergasted. Throughout the pregnancy no one had given me any indication that I was carrying two babies. I was amazed, but I was also discouraged because the doctors told us that neither one of them would live.

"When they let Van see me for the first time after the birth his face was as red as a rose. He'd wanted a son and now he had two of them. But it was a difficult time for us because, although we were both so pleased to have twin sons, we had little hope they would survive.

"Aside from being seven weeks premature, Dick had a problem resulting from Rh negative blood. Just before he'd been born my body had taken most of the blood from his and he needed transfusions to keep him alive. When I was strong enough to go home they both were still in critical condition. I had to leave the hospital without them. I'll never forget looking at them in their incubators before I left. Both had big frames, but their skin just hung on their bodies. The image of those emaciated babies stayed with me for a long time. During the next couple of weeks, I almost wished the hospital hadn't let me see them at all. I'd never been more depressed."

Despite weighing less than five pounds each, both boys had resilient hearts. As the weeks passed they began to put on weight and little by little they grew stronger. "We'd come and look at them, but they wouldn't let me touch or nurse them. The doctors told us that their immune systems were quite weak and that any contact with germs would likely kill them," Hilda recalls. "After six weeks Tom finally got to come home. I hadn't touched that child since giving birth to him and it was a little strange and frightening to hold him---but it was wonderful too.

"The doctor had said he wanted me to bring them

home one at a time because he thought I'd have my hands full. I've never been afraid of hard work and I was eager to have them both with us, but the doctor was right. When Dick came home about all I had time for was feeding and changing diapers. They required a lot of attention, but they were good babies. During their early months they didn't cry much or keep us up at night, but by the end of the year they were walking and were into everything. One would go one way and the other would go in the other direction. They kept me on my toes, but having them with us made Van and me happy."

The twins continued to grow and by their first birthday it became apparent that they were not going to be puny guys who get sand kicked in their faces. At age three they were larger than any of the other toddlers their age and, by the time they started school, they looked as though they belonged in the third grade rather than the first. Even more amazing was the fact that the two were literally indistinguishable.

"Van and I had a difficult time telling them apart," Hilda admits. "They looked exactly alike and it seemed that they each reached the different stages of development at about the same time. For example, they both started walking by their tenth month, which is when most babies start walking, but they were both late in learning how to talk. I believe that was because they had a language of their own."

"We tried to treat them as equally as we could. I'd make sure they each received the same amount of attention and tried to see that they both got the same serving size of food and so on. For a long time, I even dressed them in matching outfits. I suppose I might have carried this a bit too far. I've heard that the experts disagree with doing it that way, but the boys seemed to

Hilda Van Arsdale with Dick and Tom at 20 months.

Boy Scouts Dick and Tom with their trusty dog Pal.

have turned out just fine."

Dick and Tom were first introduced to athletics by their father who would come home after school and take the boys to his track practices. "They'd sit up in the stands all bundled up while Van ran his practices," says Hilda. "Van used to laugh about that. He said they'd sit there like two statues. They wouldn't move an inch."

As is often the case in Indiana, Tom and Dick weren't very old before they were introduced to the game of basketball. When they were five, their grandfather, Bert Van Arsdale, put a backboard and bucket up in their backyard and shortly thereafter Dick and Tom fell in love with the game. "My earliest basketball memories are of the hoop Grandfather put up in the back yard and of the state basketball tournament which we watched on TV," recalls Tom. "Our neighbors, the Davises, had a television set and I think the first game we ever saw on television was an I.U. game. Later, when our parents got a television, Dick and I would watch state tournament games with our scorebooks in hand and keep track of the scoring."

"We loved basketball and sometimes it wasn't just the game that was so appealing, it was all of the hoopla surrounding the game as well. One of the funniest things we ever saw was Tim O'Neill standing on his head in downtown Greenwood. Tim was a sportswriter from Johnson County. He once made the comment that if Greenwood High School could beat Franklin then he'd stand on his head in the middle of downtown Greenwood. Well, it happened---Greenwood beat Franklin and Dick and I got to watch Tim make good on his bet."

One of the first and most memorable games the twins attended was the Milan-Muncie Central championship in 1954. The game was a classic confrontation between a small town high school, Milan, and a big city school which had already won several state championships. (The Milan-Muncie game was the inspiration for "Hoosiers," the successful motion picture.) The twins had a "front row" seat to that contest. "Dad was a ticket-taker at the fieldhouse and he'd let Tom and I tag along to watch the games," Dick recalls. "I don't think either one of us will ever forget that Milan-Muncie game. We sat on the rubber mat the players used to clean off their feet before taking the floor and we had a great view of the game. I don't remember a lot of the details, but Bobby Plump's game winning basket is in my mind like it happened yesterday. The excitement that night was something else. Every day after that we dreamed of playing for a state championship."

The twins got their first taste of organized basketball while they were in the fifth grade where, much taller and more talented than their classmates, Tom and Dick were promoted to the seventh grade team. In their first game, Tom scored eleven points and Dick was close behind with seven. Tom remembers that game well. "We were both a little nervous because we were younger than the guys with whom we were playing and it was our first game. Prior to that it had just been me against Dick or an occasional pick-up game with the neighbors. I think we both thought it would be tougher than it was. Except for the nerves, playing against an opponent was a heck of a lot easier than going against Dick. That was one of the few games Mom and Dad did not attend and we couldn't wait to get home and tell them about our success."

The twins had many more successful outings, but they both remember one particular game in their early careers that they'd just as soon forget. "In seventh grade we played a game against St. Marks," Dick explains. "They whipped us 53-14 and neither Tom nor I scored a point. Mom was driving us home from that game and when she pulled up to one of the stoplights in Greenwood Dad said: `I can't stand to be riding in a car with two guys who don't have the pride to work any harder than you two did tonight.' Then he got out of the car and walked home."

"That stung us," Tom adds. "We loved our father and didn't like it when he was disappointed in us. I think that was one of the more drastic things that he did, but he and Mom were great motivators. They were involved in our young lives and they encouraged us to give one hundred percent in everything we did."

Lloyd Coverstone, the twins' basketball coach during their early years, remembers Dick and Tom as a couple of young phenoms. "They were outstanding athletes and good students. And they had great parents. Mr. and Mrs. Van Arsdale attended almost all of the games and they always sat at the top of the bleachers. They never interfered and it meant a lot to me that they would trust me to teach their talented boys how to succeed in basketball.

"When the twins were in the sixth grade, they were a head taller than everybody except for one young lady who was about four inches taller than either one of them," Lloyd adds. "In addition to height, they both were extremely gifted athletes. You expect tall gangly youngsters to be uncoordinated, but such was not the case with Tom and Dick. As sixth graders they played on my eighth grade team. Greenwood was a small town so we usually were the whipping boys for all of the other county schools, but with Dick and Tom we were tough. I'll never forget the first time I put them out on the floor. We were playing Ninevah who was coached by a friend of mine, Dick Thile. The game wasn't even four minutes old before the twins had completely taken over. Thile just leaned out from the bench down the floor and gave me this `where-did-these-guys-come-from' look.

"Another thing that stands out in my mind about the twins is that they were both fierce competitors. They hated to lose. One year we went all the way to the finals of the county tournament and then lost to Trafalgar in the final game. You should have seen those kids cry. You'd thought they'd just lost the world championship. They played basketball with their hearts on their sleeves and when they lost they took it very hard."

Basketball was not the only sport in which the twins would distinguish themselves. They played baseball and ran track as well. In fact, a baseball game was the scene of one of the twins most memorable pranks involving their similar identities. "We played baseball on the same team," Tom recalls. "And the only way that they could tell us apart was by putting a green cap on Dick and a red cap on me. We were playing an important game and it was my turn to pitch. But I had a sore arm. The way the rules worked, if you were not designated as a pitcher you were not supposed to pitch, and if you were designated as a pitcher you could only pitch so many innings per week. All of our pitchers had pitched their innings except for me, and I didn't want to pitch because my arm was sore.

"Dick was not a designated pitcher, but he could pitch about as well as me. We knew that, except for our hats, no one could tell us apart, so we went behind the dugout and traded hats. Dick pitched the entire game and no one ever even suspected that we had switched."

The baseball incident was one of the rare situations where the twins took advantage of their similar appearances. They looked so much alike that cases of mistaken identity occurred almost daily, yet they had the

Identical twins in identical outfits. Tom is on the left and Dick is on the right (I think).

good sense to avoid making this situation any worse than what it was.

Of course, being look alikes on the basketball court sometimes gave them a natural advantage. "If a team was playing us man-to-man inevitably Tom or I would end up with two guys guarding us," says Dick. "We both managed to get a lot of easy baskets that way and sometimes it was funny to listen to our opponents arguing over who was who."

At home cases of mistaken identity were not uncommon and, in some instances, led to undeserving reprimands or punishment. "Once I hit one of the neighbor kids with a rock," Tom recalls. "He ran home and told his dad and I ran home and hid. A few minutes later an unsuspecting Dick got yelled at for doing something that he didn't do. Things like that didn't happen very often, but when they did one or the other of us usually ended up being mad as heck."

"If one of them did something wrong we'd spank the both of them," Hilda explains when asked to describe how she and her husband handled discipline with two youngsters who looked exactly alike. "We had trouble telling them apart so if one did something wrong then they both got punished---but they were good kids so discipline was not much of a problem."

* *

By the time Tom and Dick were ready to enter high school, they'd become two of the best athletes in Greenwood. While the coaches at Greenwood High School looked forward to having the twins on their teams, Hilda and Raymond Van Arsdale had different plans for their identical sons. "We wanted them to have the best educational and athletic situation we could make available to them," says Hilda. "Greenwood is a fine community and they had a great high school, but we felt the level of competition and overall academic environment would be better at Emmerich Manual High School where Van taught and I worked as an assistant to the vice-principal. Manual was in the Indianapolis school system so we had to pay tuition, but we thought it was well worth it."

"I know we hurt some people's feelings and ruffled a few feathers when we enrolled the boys at Manual, but we had to do what we thought was best for them."

Greenwood residents, as ardent high school basketball fans as any other small town residents, rued the loss of two such fine athletes. The town made a legal inquiry to be certain that the Van Arsdales were paying to have their children educated in the Indianapolis school system. Others suggested that Hilda's job at Manual was part of a payoff for having the twins attend school there. As is often the case in situations such as this, the issue was hot for a few weeks and then cooled in the minds of most while quietly smoldering with those who are more easily given to complaining.

"We always knew we were going to attend Manual," asserts Dick. "I'm sure some people didn't like that, but we didn't hear many complaints. I don't think we lost any friends because of it. Mom and Dad did the right thing and anyone else in the same position would probably have done the same thing."

*Dick (left), Tom (right) with their mother on the
shores of Lake Superior.*

*Dick and Tom with their cousins Mike and Ole Thomas
at their grandparents farm.*

Chapter 2

Ary Skillman of New Salem, Indiana congratulates Tom (left) and Dick (right) on winning the Trester Award. (photo courtesy of Indianapolis Star)

By the time Tom and Dick entered high school, they both had a burning desire to play college basketball. Dick believes that family members helped steer them towards such a goal. "Our Uncle John went to Indiana University. He knew Branch McCracken and Lou Watson who coached basketball there. Uncle John and several other family members were avid fans of Indiana University basketball. Their enthusiasm rubbed off on Tom and me," Dick explains. "When we were growing up, many of our heroes were college and professional players and, for as long as I can remember, we wanted to play college basketball."

"It was almost an obsession," Tom admits. "We had basketball pennants from the professional league and all kinds of basketball photos hanging up in our room. Dick and I played every day and watched as many games as we could.

We were fortunate because some of the best players in the state, players such as Willie Gardner, Hallie Bryant, Bailey Robertson, and Oscar Robertson, played at Crispus Attucks in Indianapolis. They played many of their games at Butler University and we went to as many as we could. Attucks had won back-to-back state championships and played an exciting brand of basketball. The team always had great athletes. They played basketball at a level far above that of most of their competition. After watching them play we had a better idea as to how much work we had to do if we wanted to be able to compete against the better players.

Accomplishments in any arena of endeavor do not come without a price. Inevitably the best and the brightest in any field achieve such a standing by allocating a substantial amount of time and effort, while neglecting other pursuits. Such was certainly the case with Dick and Tom. "We were taller and a little quicker than most guys, and we had talent," explains Dick. "But I don't think we would have done as well as we did if not for the hours and hours we spent practicing."

Of course, an additional benefit was the natural competition created between two like-minded individuals. From the basketball court to the classroom, the twins challenged each other to be the best. "If we went out to play one-on-one and Dick won, then I was determined to play him until I won," Tom recalls. "Sometimes it got to the point where one of us would let the other win the game because we didn't want to miss dinner."

"When they went at each other on the basketball court it was something to watch," recalls Garry Donna, a friend and rival who played across town at Cathedral High School. "They played hard, physical ball and it made you cringe to imagine trying to stop either one of them. I think they went harder at each other than they did anyone else." While this might have been the case, the twins cannot ever recall losing a two-on-two contest in which they were both on the same team.

"It wasn't any fair to have both of them on the same team," says John `Ole' Thomas, a cousin from Huntington who now practices medicine in Pocatello, Idaho. "Whenever they came into town or when our family visited them, we'd play a few games against Tom and Dick. The scores would end up something like 21-3. If they were really off the score might have been 21-10. They were big, quick, tough, and they hated to get scored on. When they played on separate teams you'd catch yourself standing and watching them go at it.

"The first time I played ball with them was on our grandfather's farm. He had a basket up in the hay loft. We were about five years old, and Dick and Tom were already better at basketball than any of the rest of us. They were talented, but they worked hard too." The twin's work ethic and talent placed them in a unique position. Before they'd even played in their first high school game, the press had begun touting them as two of the better players in the state. Of course, they received additional scrutiny because of their identical appearance, but that attention did not distract them from their objective. And, while their ultimate goal was to become college basketball players, their immediate future was built around helping the Manual Redskins win a state championship.

"We'd watched the state tournament for years. Dad worked at the fieldhouse as a ticket-taker and he'd let us in and we'd sit on the edge of the floor and watch the games," Tom recalls. "Every time we went the stands were packed and the atmosphere was charged with excitement. Dick and I wanted to play in a state championship as much as two young men can want anything---and we were more than willing to do the work to get there."

In addition to their dedication to basketball, the twins were involved in other sports and participated in numerous school-sponsored clubs and social functions. During their freshman year, Dick and Tom went out for the freshman football team. Dick played split end and Tom played quarterback. The freshman team had a 7-0 record. The twins greatest moment came when Dick caught a fifty-one-yard touchdown pass thrown by Tom. "When I dropped back into the pocket, I had a pretty good idea as to where Dick would be, so he was the only receiver I was looking for. As soon as I saw him break free from his defender, I threw the ball. I figured if I got it close he'd catch it and he did."

Tom and Dick enjoyed football, but played only one season. "We didn't want to risk an injury," explains Dick. "Besides the football season didn't end until right before basketball season started and we needed to be preparing for basketball more than we needed to be members of the football team."

As freshman the twins played on the freshman, junior varsity, and varsity basketball teams. Their freshman team went undefeated. They played sporadically with the junior varsity squad and participated in seven varsity contests, including brief stints in the sectional during the state tournament. "We were surprised that Coach Cummins dressed us for the sectional because freshman almost never got to go to the state tournament," Tom recalls. "We not only got to go---we got to play a little too. That's a bittersweet memory for me because I wanted to play, but I had a bruised thigh and I could barely get around on it without a lot of pain. When Coach Cummins put me in the game I could hardly wait for him to take me out."

In 1958 Manual lost in the sectional against Broad Ripple, bringing to an end the twins' first season as high school basketball players. Later that spring they competed in track and baseball and concentrated on their studies. By the end of the year, they had not only distinguished themselves as two fine athletes, they were straight "A" students as well. During the summer they continued to work on their basketball skills and dreamed about playing for a state championship.

As sophomores Dick and Tom started at forward on the varsity team. During the next three seasons they would become two of the best players in the state. The twins, along with Ron Wood, a 5'9" guard who could score from anywhere on the floor, helped lead the Redskins to an upset victory over highly-rated Indianapolis Shortridge. Manual even came close to eventual state champion, Crispus Attucks. The Redskins closed their season with a four-point loss to Southport and then had to face Southport again in the final of the sectional.

The tournament contest was even closer than the regular season affair. The two teams battled for four quarters. Manual held a 41-39 advantage with less than a minute to play, but Southport's Leland Richards tied the game with a shot from the perimeter, forcing an overtime. The two teams stayed even through the three minute overtime. Then, with only two seconds remaining, Southport's Dan Woerner went up for a shot and was fouled. He hit both free throws to give Southport a two point lead. The game ended with Dick tossing a sixty-foot desperation heave. His shot put lumps in the throats of Southport fans, but it missed by about an inch, bouncing off the left side of the rim.

The overtime loss was a tough pill to swallow, but as the twins would learn it was not the end of the world. "I don't know why we always seemed to be involved in those close games," says Dick shaking his head. "It hurts like hell when you lose a close one, but when you lose one like that you have to believe that if you work a little harder you might win the next one."

* *

During their junior season Tom and Dick were already being pursued by college recruiters. In a pre-season article, the *Indianapolis Star* reported that the twins had received over forty letters from colleges and universities seeking to recruit them for their basketball programs. Tom acknowledges that there was a lot of interest from colleges. "We had inquiries from such basketball powerhouses as Duke and Kentucky. John Wooden had just arrived at UCLA and he wanted us to come out there and play. The Air Force Academy and Army both wanted us. We even had a letter from Columbia. But we really weren't too concerned or much involved with the recruiting. Our parents took care of that end of it. Dick and I kept our focus on school and basketball." While their parents and coach kept the recruiters at bay, the twins and their teammates worked at raising the level of their play. "During the summer, the other guys on the team and I would go to Greenwood to play with Tom and Dick in their backyard," recalls Jim Cummings, a guard on the Manual team. "Sometimes Dick, Tom, and I would play in Indianapolis at the dustbowl or at this house on 21st and Hawthorne. I don't remember whose house it was, but every week a lot of the good players from around the area would come out there and play. I remember when we went to Boy's State (a honor camp for high school students) we'd sneak off and play pick-up games in the gym. One year the three of us were playing together and some of the other guys were in awe of the fact that the three of us would be playing for the same school."

Hallie Bryant, a former Crispus Attucks superstar and member of the Harlem Globetrotters, remembers seeing the twins play at the dustbowl during their early years. "When you played ball at the dustbowl you soon discovered that there are two kinds of players: Those who are afraid and those who aren't. Dick and Tom were not afraid. They wanted to play against the best competition and they didn't back down when the pressure was on. Some guys are great players when their team is winning, but when the game gets tight they disappear. Other guys seem to thrive on that pressure. Dick and Tom could play it both ways. They were always in the thick of it."

"I think playing basketball with guys like Hallie

Bryant, Willie Gardner, Bobby Jo Edmunds, Bill Hampton, Ed Scearcy, and the other great players from Lockefield and the Fall Creek YMCA helped us to realize how intense the game can be played," explains Dick. "Hallie Bryant had this cross step fake that could fool anybody---and he'd follow it with a slashing drive to the basket. We learned a lot about driving to the basket from him. Willie Gardner was a great big man. If not for heart problems he would have given Wilt and Bill Russell plenty of problems. Willie was 6'8" or so and he weighed over two hundred pounds, but he had great agility. He made moves to the basket and inventive dunk shots long before such shots were popular in the pros. Oscar's older brother Bailey had a hell of a jump shot. In fact, most of the guys, even the big guys like Edmunds and Scearcy were absolutely deadly from about seventeen feet in.

"Every time we went down to the Avenue we came home having seen a few unbelievable plays. On the play grounds guys tend to try a few things they won't try when a coach is watching. And the guys who played at the dustbowl or at Fall Creek were inventing new moves almost every time they played. Most of the players there were black and I think they kinda looked down their noses at a lot of the white players who weren't quite as athletic. Tom and I considered ourselves lucky to be invited to play. Having the opportunity to play against such talent all summer long was a great learning experience."

* *

The 1960 Manual Redskins got off to one of the school's best starts in many years. They turned more than a few heads when they toppled state champions Crispus Attucks (64-57) in the semifinal of the Indianapolis City Tournament. They lost in the final to

Arsenal Tech (54-51), but later avenged that loss, shelling the Greenclads 64-46. In that second meeting, the twins accounted for thirty-seven (Tom scored 19, Dick, 18) of their team's sixty-four points.

As the season progressed, the Redskin starting five, which, in addition to Tom and Dick, included senior Roger Wood and juniors Larry Short and Jim Cummings, began to show incredible shooting accuracy. Against Greenfield in late January, for example, they hit for over fifty-eight percent from the field. A key to the Redskins' shooting success was the physical play of the Van Arsdales. The twins were able to drive close to the basket where they would pass the ball to an open teammate if they were double covered, or take a shot if one was available. Without the ball they set wicked picks for their teammates, enabling the Redskins to take many shots within ten feet of the basket. The twins and Larry Short were also strong rebounders. Fighting for inside position, they were able to get additional chances for easy baskets by rebounding their teammate's errant shots.

In fact, much of Manual's offense was built around the twins' abilities. Even so, their teammates recall them as unselfish players who were much more concerned about winning basketball games than they were about being top scorers. Manual fans also point to the twins' unselfish play between themselves. "I think they tried as hard as they could to see that they and everybody else on the team had an equal opportunity to score," recalls Jimmie Angelopoulous, a reporter for the *Indianapolis Times*. "But Dick and Tom were so talented I think that sometimes worked against them. It was admirable that they were so unselfish, especially when it came to getting each other the ball. But I've always wondered how many points one or the other could have scored if the other one wasn't around."

Apparently Coach Cummins wondered about this too. "One night before a game Coach Cummins came up to me in the lockerroom. He said: `Dick, I want you to go out there tonight and break the school scoring record.' He then added that he didn't want me to tell Tom that he'd asked me to do this. That night I scored thirty-one points which tied the school scoring record (set by Dick Nyers in 1952)." The Redskins beat a good Warren Central team that night by twenty-six points (79-53).

A week later, Tom was getting dressed for a game against Howe when Coach Cummins approached him. He told Tom to go out that night and break the school scoring record. Cummins asked Tom to not mention their discussion to Dick. Tom went out and scored thirty-two points---the last two coming on a couple of free throws with Manual way out in front and only a few minutes remaining."

"I'll never forget it," recalls Larry Short who was on the floor for Manual when Tom broke the record. "Tom had tied Dick's record with the first free throw and he looked over at Coach Cummins before the second one as if to ask: You really want me to do this? Cummins just nodded his head and Tom hit another to set the record."

With ample help from the Van Arsdales, the 1960 Manual Redskins approached the post-season tournament with a sparkling 22-3 record. They were favored to win the Southport sectional. The Redskins coasted to a 62-44 win against Greenfield in the opening round, but then struggled against Franklin Township. Manual had to hit six of their first nine shots in the fourth quarter to post a 58-53 victory. "We played miserably," confessed Coach Cummins to the Indianapolis press. Cummins went on to say he hoped his boys would be able to turn things around in the championship game against Southport.

The evening's finale featured a red-hot shooting exhibition from the Van Arsdales, Roger Wood, and the entire Redskin team. Manual hit fifty-three percent of their shots in posting a convincing 71-61 victory over Southport. The win was sweet revenge for the previous season's loss and sent the Redskins to a regional for the first time in thirty-seven years. "Winning the sectional is a thrilling experience," Dick explains. "Even though it's only the first of the four steps in winning a state championship, it's still one of the most rewarding because you play several games over three days and the guys you're playing against are from around the area. I think winning the sectional gave us a lot of confidence. That confidence would carry over into the next season."

With a sectional title under their belts, the Redskins spent the following week preparing for North Salem and hoping for a return match-up against Tech, who had whipped Cathedral in the Indianapolis sectional. Manual mauled North Salem (71-51) in the afternoon contest and Tech also advanced, setting up an all-Indianapolis regional final. The game would be the third meeting between the two schools and most observers agreed that both teams were as close to equal as two teams could be.

The game was a closely fought affair. The score was tied ten times and there were fifteen lead changes. The last lead change came in the waning seconds of the game and became the subject of a great deal of controversy. With fourteen seconds left, Manual held a 45-42 advantage. Tech quickly brought the ball up the court and got it into the able hands of Melvin Garland. Garland, a 6'3" all-state guard, had been having a terrible day. Earlier he'd hit only one of his first eighteen field goal attempts, but in the fourth quarter he'd caught fire.

On this critical possession, he canned a corner jumper and then he and his teammates quickly went into a full court press, now trailing by only one point.

Manual safely in-bounded the ball and tried to move it up court against the hacking Tech defense. With only seconds remaining, Tom had possession of the ball and, moving across the center line, he collided with Garland who had blocked his path When the two collided the referee blew his whistle. For a spilt second the fieldhouse fell silent. Then the referee, Marvin Todd, gave the signal for an offensive foul. The moment the call was made Coach Cummins came storming off the bench with every Manual fan loudly complaining along with him. Their protest, however, fell on deaf ears and Garland was awarded a chance to hit two free throws. He nailed them both, giving Tech a 46-45 victory.

"Mel Garland was a great player, but he was even a better actor," Tom contends. "We'd played them three times and every time we did Mel would try to fake the refs into calling a charge by flopping backwards and falling to the floor when you got close to him. Most refs could tell he was faking, but for some reason Todd didn't. You have to give Garland credit for hitting those free throws under pressure, but he ought to get an Oscar for the acting performance he pulled at mid-court."

Dick doesn't want fans to think that he and Tom were always complaining about the officials, but he does believe that their physical style of play earned them a few bad calls along the way. "We always seemed to get the short end of those situations. Tom and I were bigger and more physical than a lot of the guys we played against and I don't think we got the benefit of the doubt very much. During the season calls such as the one made against Tom in the regional were something we learned to shake off, but this one came in the last seconds of a tournament game. We'd lost in the last seconds to Southport in the sectional during our sophomore year and to lose a close game on free throws for the second time in as many years was extremely disappointing."

* *

The disappointment of losing in the state tournament, while not an easy thing to forget, was something Dick and Tom were able to put behind them. After the basketball season they both competed in track. Tom set a school record in the shot put (53'4"), while Dick broke the city record in the high hurdles (15.0 seconds).

In the classroom the Van Arsdales continued to carry "A" averages. In fact, their enthusiasm for academics carried over to some of their classmates. "Dick and Tom were leaders, but not in the way you usually imagine leaders to be," recalls Ann Cummins, wife of Manual coach Dick Cummins. "They were shy young men who did not talk a lot. They led by example. One of the things my husband was most proud of was the fact that six of the seniors on the 1961 basketball team were members of the National Honor Society. He always believed that Dick and Tom were partly responsible for that."

"They challenged me athletically and scholastically," agrees fellow teammate Jim Cummings. "The twins and I were in the same grade so they were in many of my classes. They paid careful attention to their studies and were disappointed if they did not do well. Their attitudes rubbed off on me. I graduated thirty-fourth in my class and I don't believe I would have done as well if not for the competition we shared in the classroom. Dick and Tom helped me realize that academics are as important as athletics."

"They set the tone for our entire graduating class,"

adds Sherry (Braun) Kerner Shemons, a classmate and one of Dick's closest high school friends. "Seeing two such fine athletes devoted to doing well in the classroom made a great impression on the rest of us. So many times star athletes try to slide through on the academic end, but not the twins. They worked as hard in their studies as they did on their basketball. It was fun to be involved with them in friendly academic competition. The good grades always felt a little better if you knew you'd done better than the Van Arsdales."

Lest anyone be inclined to think that Dick and Tom were two perfect angels---they were also known to have been involved in their fair share of shenanigans. "We were far from perfect," Tom confesses. "I think one of the stupidest things we did as kids happened one night when Dick and I were out in our parents' car, cruising on the south side of Indianapolis. In those days the Dairy Queen had small cones you could buy for a nickel. We bought a couple dozen and started driving around, looking for places to toss them. We found a guy over by Garfield Park, he must have been necking with his girlfriend or something. Anyway, we lobbed these cones in through the windows of his car and he came popping up in the seat madder than a hornet."

"We got out of there as fast as we could," says Dick, picking up the story. "But this guy was one of those people who just loved his car. He was determined to catch us. We almost got away, but then Tom pulled us into a dead end street and we were trapped.

"We were pretty big guys and we knew we could handle ourselves, but when this fellow got out of his car he was holding a big hay hook. He walked around to the front of our car, and suddenly our night on the town was not so fun. We were in our parents brand new car and this guy was threatening to smash a hay hook through the hood of it. Tom and I were practically on our knees begging him not to do it. The only way we got out of that mess was by cleaning up the inside of his car. We'd started off that night thinking we were going to raise a little hell, but by the time we got home we were just happy to be returning our parents' car without a hay hook sticking out of its hood."

When the twins weren't playing basketball or terrorizing the neighborhood with miniature ice cream cones, they occasionally went out on a date. "We were interested in girls," Tom admits. "But we were shy and we didn't believe in going steady or anything like that. We'd double date for dances or the prom."

"When we were freshman a couple of girls, Barbara Emmrich and Jenny Perry asked us out to a dance," Dick adds. "I think that was our first date. We couldn't drive so our parents had to pick us up and take us home. We probably looked like a couple of farm kids that night."

"All I can remember about that date was that we'd slow dance, but there was no way we were going to try those fast dances."

"I'd say they were a little backward in that area," assesses Larry Short, a good friend and basketball teammate. "Once, on a bus ride to New Albany for a basketball game, a couple of us felt inclined to give them both a little pep talk and a few pointers as to how to handle the girls," Short adds with a grin. "As I recall they were both a little shy about such things."

While the twins might have been shy around the opposite sex they showed no timidness whatsoever when it came time to play basketball. And, as their senior season began, the pair began to dominate games in a fashion seldom seen in high school basketball. "They were two of the most rugged players I've ever seen," recalls Marvin Wood, the Milan mentor who was coaching at Indianapolis North Central while Dick and Tom were in high school. "One night one of my kids came streaking down court for a breakaway layup and one of those twins managed to get in front of him and take a swat at his shot. Whoever it was stopped the ball with his hand but my player just kept on coming. His feet went out from under him and he landed on his butt. They made plays like that all night long. It was bad enough to have to face one guy like that, but two of them was too much."

"I've always thought that Joe Sexson was the greatest all-around athlete ever to come out of Indianapolis," says Ray Crowe, who guided Crispus Attucks to consecutive state championships and coached several of the game's greatest players, including Oscar Robertson. "I rank Dick and Tom about equal to Sexson. They were big, quick, and they had mental toughness. During their junior and senior seasons, they could control any game they played."

In 1961, the twins along with fellow seniors Jim Cummings, Armen Cobb, and Larry Short, dominated their opponents on the basketball court. Manual lost only two games during the entire season. They dropped the first game of the season against Indianapolis Cathedral. The Irish rode fine performances from Walt Sahm and Gary Donna to a 63-53 victory. The Redskins second loss came against Crispus Attucks (59-54) in the final of the city tournament. In compiling a 19-2 regular-season, the twins and their teammates posted impressive victories over highly-regarded New Albany (79-54) and Columbus (71-55). They avenged their regional loss to Tech (61-54) and closed out the season with a great display of defense in disposing Scecina 72-32.

Manual was heavily favored to win the Southport

sectional. The only thing that nearly stopped them was the weather. A blizzard hit the state during the 1961 state tournament's first weekend. Dumping a blanket of snow over two feet deep in places, the blizzard forced the postponement of many games and left spectators and participants stranded at tournament sites from Whiting to Watson. For Manual's opponents at the Southport sectional, the snow could only provide a brief reprieve. The Redskins clobbered all four of their sectional opponents: New Palestine (64-44), Greenfield (76-49), Franklin Central (61-35), and Vernon Township (58-41). Manual's margin of victory averaged over twenty points, but trouble lay ahead in the regional where, if they could get by Plainfield, they would probably meet Crispus Attucks in the final.

Plainfield was no match for the taller and more talented Manual quintet. The Quakers fell 66-54. Attucks beat Alexandria, setting up a return meeting with the Redskins, whom they'd beaten in the tourney by five points. Attucks came into the contest carrying the state's #3 ranking, while Manual was rated fifth in the statewide poll. While the Van Arsdales represented Manual's best, Attucks featured 6'8" center Bill Jones and an excellent perimeter-shooting guard Jerry Trice.

Manual led 13-8 at the end of the first quarter, but disaster struck in the second as the Redskins missed all thirteen of their field goal attempts, permitting Attucks to take a three- point lead into the lockerroom at halftime. Trailing 22-19 at the start of the third period, Manual, behind the one-two punch of Dick and Tom Van Arsdale, started hitting shots from the outside and scored nine straight points for a 28-22 lead midway through the third. As Attucks was forced to extend its defense, the twins were able to use a double post, earning them numerous shots close to the basket. The Tigers were unable to contain the inside-outside threat and fell in a shocking 55-44 upset. The twins combined for forty-five points--- one more than the entire Attucks team.

"Beating Crispus Attucks in the regional was quite an accomplishment," says Dick. "The school had a great basketball tradition. They'd won several state championships and it seemed like they had great teams every year. When we lost to them in the city tournament, I figured they might be the toughest team we'd face all year. Beating them in the regional gave us confidence. I think that game---more than any other---showed us that we could play with anyone."

In the semi-state the Redskins would need every shred of confidence they could muster. For the second time in as many weeks they won their afternoon contest without much difficulty. They whipped Connersville 61-49 and faced Muncie Central in the evening's finale. Muncie, a perennial tournament powerhouse with five state championships to its credit, had been the runners-up in the previous year's tourney and hoped to find its way into the final four for the second time in as many years. Manual, making the school's first trip to a semi-state final in thirty-nine years, was not impressed with the Bearcat's credentials as they pulled away to a 42-30 halftime lead.

In the second half, Muncie clawed their way back behind an outstanding performance from Gerald Lanich. Lanich scored thirteen points in the second half and pulled the Bearcats into 54-54 tie with a little over two minutes remaining in the game. Manual, however, was not to be denied. Dick put them back into the lead 56-54 and the Redskins held on for a thrilling 62-59 victory.

Manual's win put them into the final four to face Tell City. The state's #1 ranked team, Kokomo, would face

Logansport in the other afternoon contest, with the winners meeting later in the evening to decide the state champion for 1961. Most observers believed that Manual and Kokomo would be playing in that final game. Such was the case as Manual overcame a great shooting display by Tom Kron (Kron later played for Seattle and St. Louis in the NBA). The Redskins scalped Tell City 70-55 and Kokomo beat Logansport 86-77.

The 1961 state final featured two teams with contrasting styles. Kokomo had two fine outside shooting forwards in Ron Hughes and Richie Scott. The Kats outside shooting was augmented by Jim Ligon, a 6'7" center who was quite capable at rebounding errant shots and putting them back in the basket. Manual, on the other hand, hoped to achieve their objectives by getting the ball inside to Dick and Tom. The Redskins coveted shots from fifteen feet in.

Both teams were nervous at the start. Manual held a slim 13-12 advantage the end of the first quarter, but then the twins began to dominate the game and the Redskins pulled out to a 35-28 halftime lead. In the third quarter, Tom owned the backboards. Grabbing nearly every rebound in sight, he kept Kokomo from getting more than one shot at the basket. Unfortunately, his teammates were struggling with their shooting and the Redskins saw their seven point lead cut to 43-42 by the end of the stanza. While Tom's aggressive play helped him to lead both teams with eighteen rebounds, he found himself saddled with three fouls. He committed his fourth foul with a little over five minutes left. Then, with less than three minutes to play, Tom made a drive for the basket. His shot went in, giving Manual a 57-53 lead---but no sooner had the ball left his hand when the referee blew his whistle indicating that Tom had committed a charging foul. Coach Cummins and every Manual supporter in the stadium raised their voice in protest, but to no avail.

"I couldn't believe that it was happening to me again," says Tom. "I've watched films of the game on several occasions and I honestly don't believe I charged on that play. One of the hardest things I've ever had to do was to go sit on the bench after that foul and watch my team try to win the game."

With Tom gone from the lineup, Manual shifted into a slow-down offense to try and protect their four point lead. Kokomo responded by abandoning their zone in favor of a man-to-man defense. This shift in strategy quickly resulted in a Kokomo foul, which sent Jim Cummings to the line for a one and one. He hit both ends, expanding Manual's lead to 59-53. Kokomo managed to cut the lead to three (62-59) with :49 showing on the clock and then forced a jump ball on Manual's next possession. Kokomo controlled the tip and got the ball down low to Jim Ligon who was fouled by Larry Short. Ligon hit one free throw to pull the Wildcats within two (62-60).

With less than twenty seconds on the clock, Kokomo used a full court press which enabled them to force another jump ball. The tip was controlled by Jim Cummings, who was immediately "tied-up" by Ron Hughes, requiring yet another jump ball. Kokomo garnered the tip and Richie Scott, who along with Ron Hughes had caught fire from the outside, drained a twenty footer tieing the game at sixty-two.

In the last ten seconds, the Redskins got the ball into Dick Van Arsdale's able hands. Dick would lead all scorers that night with twenty-four points, but his last-second lean-in jumper hit the back of the rim and bounced out. "From where I was sitting it looked like that shot was going to catch nothing but net," Tom recalls. With time about to expire, the referee blew his whistle. He indicated that Jim Cummings had fouled Richie Scott on the rebound, giving Scott an opportunity to win the game with no time left on the clock.

Standing alone at the free throw line, Scott calmly eyed the basket and tossed up a freebie that bounced off the back of the rim. The miss sent Scott to the floor pounding his fists in frustration and, for the first time in forty-three years, the state championship would be decided in overtime.

In the overtime Babe Pryor hit a bucket to give Kokomo a two point advantage. Dick countered with a basket for Manual and then Ron Hughes dropped another one of his bombs from the outside. On the next two possessions, Kokomo lost Richie Scott and Jim Ligon to fouls. Unfortunately, the Redskins were able to convert on only one of the free throws and still trailed 66-65 with less than a minute to play. At the :27 mark Dick was fouled again and hit a free throw to tie the game at sixty-six. Kokomo brought the ball to half court and called timeout for the purpose of setting up a final play.

It didn't take a genius to figure that the Wildcats wanted the ball in the hands of Ronnie Hughes. Hughes would score twenty points that night, hitting most of them from seventeen feet and beyond. He was the only one of Kokomo's scoring threats still in the game. When the teams converged back out on the court, the emotionally exhausted crowd was on its feet screaming for all they were worth. As expected, Kokomo immediately got the ball into Ronnie Hughes hands. He wasted little time in making his move for the basket. As Hughes drove to the lane, Armen Cobb tried to step into his path. In doing so he committed a foul. For the second time that night, a Kokomo player stood at the free throw line with the game on the line. This time that player did not miss. Hughes hit both of his free throws, giving Kokomo a 68-66 victory.

"It is impossible to put into words how much it hurt to lose that game," says Dick. "We worked for four years to get ourselves to a state final. Watching our dream of a state championship end on a pair of free throws in overtime was pure hell."

"In high school winning a state championship was the most important thing in our lives," adds Tom. "We did everything we could think of to get ourselves prepared and it was difficult to accept the fact that we'd lost. It was something we were eventually able to put behind us, but at the time our whole world came crashing in."

According to tradition, at the end of each state basketball tournament the runners-up are given their trophy and then the state champion is honored. After these awards are given, the commissioner of the Indiana High School Athletic Association announces the winner of the Arthur S. Trester award, given to the high school basketball player who best exemplifies the sportsmanship Hoosiers associate with their favorite game.

The ceremony is a joyous occasion for the victors and a true test of character for the vanquished, who must stand in front of fifteen thousand people while trying to come to terms with the biggest disappointment of their lives. The players from Manual, like so many players who had come before them, showed well in this their toughest moment. The twist of emotions, however, became especially difficult for Dick and Tom.

In 1961, for the first time in state tourney history, the board of Commissioners decided to co-award the Trester. They gave it to Tom and Dick Van Arsdale. "In looking back we both agree that the Trester Award is one of the highest honors we've ever received," Tom acknowledges. "That award was given to us for being more than just good basketball players. It was a validation of the values our parents had instilled in us and recognition for being good citizens."

"But we weren't in the greatest of moods when we got it," Dick interjects. "It is very difficult to smile and be happy about an individual accomplishment when you are dying inside because your team lost. We did not appreciate that award on the night we received it, but over the years we've come to realize that it is indeed a high honor."

Dick moves in for a layup against Kokomo's Richie Scott.
Photo by Ed Lacey, Jr., courtesy Indianapolis Star

Chapter 3

Dick and Tom with all star coach Angus Nicoson.
Photo by Frank Fisse courtesy of Indianapolis Star

Throughout the years the final game of Indiana's high school basketball tournament has drawn more spectators than either the NBA or the NCAA finals. In 1989, for example, over forty thousand fans were in attendance. For many years the event has been telecast throughout the midwest, and, more recently, ESPN has broadcast the game to the entire world. The high school students who participate in these final games perform under tremendous pressure. Many will not go on to play in college or for professional teams. Even if they do, they rarely find themselves playing for so much in front of so many.

The winners of these games carry with them a thrill that will last a lifetime, while the losers will never be able to shake those private thoughts of what might have been. As members of the second place team from 1961, Dick and Tom still carry the memory of that loss. "You can never forget it," Tom admits, "but you learn to live with it. At the time we had college and the possibility of professional careers in front of us. Looking to the future helped ease the sting of losing that game. In fact, if I'm not mistaken, Dick and I were out early on the morning after the state championship playing one-on-one.

"We were tremendously disappointed, but we'd given one hundred percent and had nothing to be ashamed of," explains Dick. "I think that loss was toughest on our fans. They had followed our fortunes for four years and had given us a tremendous amount of encouragement and support. Watching us lose and not being able to do a thing about it had to be tough on them.

"Whenever we meet with our former teammates or classmates, we inevitably end up talking about that game. Over the years we've been back to Manual for class reunions and various school functions and it is amazing how well people remember that game. Some still remember it as though it happened yesterday."

"I've never been able to watch the film of that game," admits teammate Larry Short. "Many years have passed and I've found success in other areas, but that loss still hurts. We were so close. . . ."

"Every once in awhile one of the cable networks here in Indianapolis telecasts our game with Kokomo," says Jim Cummings who, after graduating from Indiana Central, took a job with Detroit Diesel in Indianapolis. "People have called it one of the most exciting tournament games in the state's history. And, even though we lost, I still get excited when I remember the thrill of being involved in such a closely contested final."

Graduating members of the '61 team included Short, Armen Cobb, Jim Cummings, and Dave Schieb. Each went to college: Larry played some basketball at David Lipscomb in Tennessee; Jim Cummings stayed in the neighborhood to attend Indiana Central where he played for Angus Nicoson.

While the years have seen the twins and their teammates come to terms with the biggest disappointment of their childhoods, Dick Cummins, their coach, took the defeat even harder than they did. Dick died in 1990. His wife, Ann, describes the effect that state final loss had on her husband. "He'd worked so hard for four years and he wanted so much for those kids to win. When it didn't happen he fell into a deep depression. I don't believe he ever quite got over that loss. It was difficult for me to watch him struggle. He'd done such a fine job of getting them as far as he did. I know the boys thought the world of him and I was as proud as I could be of the job he'd done, but somehow that was not enough for him."

The loss so affected Cummins that he retired from coaching. The 1961 state final was the last game he ever coached. Dick describes how he and Tom felt about their coach and how they felt about his decision to leave coaching. "We've always been grateful for the influence he had on our lives. It was hard for us to see him become so depressed. I think he felt like he'd let us down. We never felt that way---not even for a moment. Coach Cummins had always made a point of emphasizing the fact that basketball is a game and that other areas of life are much more important. We were disappointed that he didn't chose to continue to coach and give that message to other players."

* *

With their high school basketball careers behind them, Tom and Dick turned their attention to the numerous offers they'd received to play college basketball. For months the newspapers had been speculating on where they would end up. Sportswriters had them going to Duke, Michigan, Kentucky, Purdue, Indiana, or Butler. The Van Arsdales, however, had settled on one school long before they made it official. Dick and Tom were headed for Indiana.

"We knew where we wanted to go," Dick admits. "We were just waiting for the right time to say it."

"During their senior year, the phone calls came almost everyday," recalls their mother. "Those college recruiters gave us a devil of a time. This fellow from Duke (Vic Bubas) got me so annoyed that I didn't even want him near the house. When Adolph Rupp came around he brought his tailor and promised Dick and Tom would get all the clothes they needed. He told us if the twins went to Kentucky he'd have Van and I flown to all of their games. I was tempted to invite him back just to see what else he might offer.

"We took the boys to visit Purdue and Michigan, but they wanted to go to IU and that was fine with us. My brother John was good friends with Branch McCracken and Lou Watson. (Branch was the head basketball coach at Indiana. Lou was his assistant. Lou later became head coach, preceding Bob Knight.) John would have been disappointed if they had chosen another school.

"Unfortunately, Indiana was on probation for violations in the football program. This meant the basketball team would be ineligible for post-season play during the boys' first three years. I suppose going to a school that was on probation might have cost them a chance to play for a national championship, but I don't think they've ever regretted choosing IU."

* *

Each year Indiana and Kentucky play a home and home all-star series featuring each state's best high school basketball players. The player awarded "Mr. Basketball" from each state wears the number "1" on his uniforms. In 1961 two players from Indiana had a "1" on their uniform: Dick and Tom Van Arsdale. As with the Trester Award, the announcement marked the first time that two players were co-awarded that title. While the Trester Award is intended to honor sportsmanship, Mr. Basketball is an honor reserved for the best basketball player in Indiana. It was a honor the twins greatly appreciated. "Being named the two best basketball players in the state was a affirmation that all of our hard work was paying off," explains Dick.

"Having been as heavily recruited as we were and then being named the best players in Indiana gave us a tremendous amount of confidence," adds Tom. "There were a lot of great players in the state that year and to be named the best of all of those players---that put us on top of the world."

While the honor of Mr. Basketball gave the twins confidence and satisfaction, it did not change their work ethic or attitudes. "They were two of the finest young men we'd ever had associated with our all-star team," claims Bill Shover, who was in charge of arranging the annual benefit contest between Kentucky and Indiana. "You did not have to be around them long before you discovered that they'd received excellent parental guidance. Their parents were exceptional people--- especially Hilda. I'll never forget the first thing I saw when I walked into her home. She had a sign next to the door. It read: Outside this house you might be a big man, but inside Hilda is the boss. . . And so she was.

"I've known the twins for many years. I've seen them do many unique things and they've always been great guys, but my favorite story about them comes from their high school days when they were playing on the all-star team. One of our players, Bobby Miles from East Chicago, had been in an automobile accident. I had the team over to visit him and some of the children there at the hospital. In those days, we gave the players money for every mile they drove getting to practice or making a public appearance. I paid each boy as I met them at the hospital. It didn't take long for that money to start burning a hole in their pockets. After visiting with the kids, the players were wandering around the souvenir shop buying junk. Dick was about to buy a candy bar or something and Tom came up to him said: `Dick put that back. Our parents work too hard for you to be wasting money on something like that.' Tom and Dick had such respect among their peers that when Dick put whatever it was that he had back, so did most of the other guys."

In the first of the two all-star games, Dick and Tom each scored twenty-six points to help lead Indiana to a 82-71 victory. They did not fare as well in the second contest. Indiana could only hit twenty-eight percent of their field goal attempts, losing 78-75. In the second game Dick scored nine, while Tom led the team with fourteen points. With the conclusion of that second all-star contest, the twins closed their high school careers. Remarkably, their high school statistics were almost as identical as their appearance: Tom scored 1350 points and Dick 1422 (Tom played four fewer games than Dick) and they each averaged about nine rebounds per game.

The twins lockers were forever sealed in their honor.
Coach Cummins and a student look on.

*Dick and Tom pose with 1961 "500" Festival Queen, Diane Hunt.
Photo courtesy of Bill Shover and Indianapolis Newspapers.*

*1961 Indiana All Stars Top Row: (Lft to Rt.) Tom, Dick, Walt Sahm,
Bill Jones, Marion Pierce, Rich Scott. Bottom Row: Rod Schwartz,
Bob Merder, Ron Hughes, Bob Purkhiser, Gene Demaree, Doug Reid,
and coach Angus Nicoson. Photo by Frank Fisse courtesy Indpls.
Star.*

Chapter 4

Dick puts up a shot during a freshman intra-squad game.
Photo by Frank Fisse courtesy Indianapolis Star.

In the decades prior to the Bobby Knight era of Indiana University basketball, Branch McCracken, another gray-haired and boisterous coach, prowled the sidelines. Graying hair and a colorful personality were not the only similarities between the two mentors. Under McCracken's tutelage, the Hoosiers won two national titles (1940 and 1953.)

However, unlike Knight, McCracken believed that basketball games should be played at a fast tempo. He coached his teams to score a lot of points as quickly as possible. McCracken believed that you cannot beat what you cannot catch. His teams were thus dubbed "The Hurrin' Hoosiers."

Dick and Tom came to Indiana during Branch's last four years as coach. Although Branch's friendship with the twins' uncle had given him an inside track at recruiting Tom and Dick, McCracken considered himself lucky to have landed these two great players. "Their uncle, John Thomas, bragged about them before they were even in high school," recalls Lou Watson, an assistant coach under McCracken. "John taught Branch and me how to fly fish and he was always talking about his identical twin nephews. He said they'd be the best two players Branch could ever have on his team. I think he was right. When Branch went to see them play he was impressed, but he didn't think we'd have much of a chance at getting them to come to Indiana. We were on probation, which greatly diminished our ability to convince good players to come here. Branch thought getting Dick and Tom to come to Indiana was his greatest recruiting job ever. If we'd had a big man while they were here, there's no telling how good we could have been."

Unfortunately, Walt Bellamy, one of the best centers ever to play at Indiana, graduated the year before the twins came to IU. In addition to Branch's woes at the center slot and the four year probation which had come as a result of recruiting infractions in the football program, McCracken's team was also without the services of Ray Pavy. Pavy, one of the most prolific scorers in the history of Indiana high school basketball, had been paralyzed from the waist down in an automobile accident. Ray would have been a backcourt mate to another big scorer, Jimmy Rayl. (In fact, Rayl and Pavy were the key participants in what many people consider the greatest scoring exhibition in Indiana high school basketball history. Pavy scored forty-five while his opponent, Rayl, scored forty-four.)

The Van Arsdales, thus, were welcome additions to Branch's team---but they would not be available until their sophomore season. When Dick and Tom earned their scholarships to Indiana, Big Ten universities were more concerned about student-athletes making the social and academic transition from high school to college than they were of an athlete's importance to the basketball team. Member schools shared the philosophy that freshman players would benefit from not being placed under the dual pressure of competing in a college classroom and on the field of play.

Today freshman participation is widespread. The transition from high school to college is made easier for modern athletes by isolating them from the rest of the student population and providing them with tutors and academic counselors not available to the general student population. "It is most unfortunate that athletes today are not expected to be a part of the student population," says Dick. "Tom and I had a wonderful time being involved with our fellow students in all aspects of college life. Let's face it---most student-athletes do not go on to compete as professionals and they should be involved in the everyday experiences they often miss while attending college on an athletic scholarship. The social experience of living day-to-day with a wide variety of personalities devoted to various pursuits, most not related to sports, is an important part of a college education."

"And it's a whole bunch of fun," adds Tom. "We joined the Sigma Alpha Epsilon fraternity during our freshman year and over our four years we became friends with a great group of guys. We loved basketball and devoted much of our time to it, but we also had a great time with our fraternity brothers. I wouldn't trade that experience for anything.".

As freshman pledges in the Sigma Alpha Epsilon Fraternity, Dick and Tom were given a variety of duties, including rising early in the morning to make sure their older fraternity brothers got up in time for class. "They kept us hopping," Tom recalls. "We were responsible for cleaning the house after parties and so on. In addition, the fraternity encouraged good study habits by having a study table at which we all had to sit for at least four hours.

"The class work was more difficult than it had been in high school, but we had developed good habits and were able to do well. It helped that we were both enrolled in some of the same classes. For example, we both had the same calculus class early in the morning so occasionally we'd take turns attending class and taking notes."

"We got into a routine for handling class work and basketball practice, but we were still a little homesick. Once we got over that we seemed to fit right in," adds Dick. "Jon McClocklin, another freshman on the basketball team, became one of our best friends. Jon played ball for Franklin and we knew about him in high school, but we didn't meet until the summer before our freshman year when we all played on a summer team. Tom Bolyard was on that team too. Tom would be our center during our sophomore year. He was a few years older than us and was largely responsible for getting us to join the Sigma Alpha Epsilon fraternity."

"I met Dick and Tom during the summer before our freshman year," explains McGlocklin, who later played for the world champion Milwaukee Bucks. "We were being rushed by the same fraternity so I saw them a lot that summer and we became friends. I remember them as two of the funniest guys I've ever met. They used to fight about everything, but I never saw them both mad at the same time. Dick generally had the worst temper. It took a lot to get Tom really mad. But I do remember one time they were arguing about something and Tom told me I'd better leave the room because he was going to sock Dick in the mouth. I got up to leave and hadn't even got the door closed before Dick came charging out of the room behind me. He said: `Moose, I'm getting out of here, Tom's really mad.'"

* *

On the basketball court, Dick and Tom immediately distinguished themselves as two fine ball players. Although they were not able to compete in games during their freshman year, the twins were able to demonstrate their skills during the intra-squad games which were played prior to the home varsity contests.

Before the opening of the Big Ten season, the freshman squad got a crack at whipping the varsity in a benefit contest for Ray Pavy. Dick and Tom played well. Scoring twenty and twenty-two points respectively, the twins led the freshman to a near upset. McCracken was forced to use his starting unit most of the game to earn a slim 81-77 victory. In the next morning's Indianapolis Times, Jim Smith quoted McCracken as saying "Man oh man, aren't those twins something? They're strong on the boards and sure can pop them from the outside. I wish we could play them right now."

* *

When Branch finally did have the twins available to play, he still started his pre-season press conference with his favorite adage. "We're the hurtin' Hoosiers this year," he told the audience for the twentieth year in a row. While Branch was given to poor-mouthing his teams in front of the press, his 62-63 squad did have a serious deficiency. They were without a big man and would have to start either 6'6" Tom Bolyard or 6'5" Jon McGlocklin at center. Aside from this one weakness, even Branch had to concede that this squad would be among the best in the Big Ten.

Jimmy Rayl, returning for his senior season, would provide consistent offense from anywhere inside the ten-second line, and, in addition to Tom and Dick, the team was loaded with good players. Tom Bolyard, for example, had become a fine forward. Bolyard, a member of Fort Wayne's state championship team from 1959, had developed a soft shooting touch from seventeen feet in. His consistent shooting and aggressive rebounding made him a force with which to be reckoned.

As the Hoosiers opened their 1962-63 campaign, all eyes were on the tow-headed twins from Indianapolis. Sports Illustrated and Life ran feature stories on them and the local newspapers constantly referred to the great things expected of Dick and Tom. "We enjoyed that attention," Dick admits. "And we felt a little pressure. We were not the type of players who go out and score a lot of points every night. The things we brought to a team had more to do with consistency. If people were going to measure us based on what we did in the first few games, then we were going to be in trouble. I think our contribution was going to be best measured by what we did in the course of our three years."

This attitude of looking at things from a wider perspective helped Dick and Tom. They played well in their sophomore season, but the team's bona fide star was, without a doubt, Jimmy Rayl. Dubbed the "Splendid Splinter" because of his slight build, Rayl had established himself as one of the best shooters the game has ever seen. Left alone from forty feet in, Rayl was absolutely uncanny. He often drew two or three defenders and received plenty of physical abuse in return for his accurate shooting.

"People will find this hard to believe, but Rayl once called five bank shots in a row from about twelve feet inside the ten- second line," Dick recalls. "It happened when I was still silly enough to think I had a chance against him in a game of horse. He was one of the best pure shooters I've ever seen."

Before the season began, Branch made one major change in the twins' roles: he put Dick in the backcourt with Rayl. Dick worked hard at this adjustment and, as the season progressed, he became quite adept at the position. "I loved it when they put some short guy on me," Dick laughs. "But the worse thing about playing guard was Rayl making me throw the ball inbounds every time. I don't think he ever threw the ball inbounds the whole time he was at Indiana."

Dick and Tom started their first collegiate game against Virginia. The Hoosiers won 90-59 in a contest where Jimmy Rayl pumped in thirty-five points, Dick scored eleven and Tom nine. The Hoosiers followed that win with an 87-76 loss against highly- regarded Drake. Against Drake IU's lack of a big man became painfully apparent. The Hoosiers were out-rebounded 58-43 and, when the game was over, Rayl (held to "just" twenty-seven points) complained that Drake had administered "the worse beating" he'd ever taken on a basketball court.

Dick and Tom were steady performers in those early games, but not as aggressive as many people had hoped. The adjustment between the high school and college game, combined with the fact that the twins had not competed in a regular game since the loss against Kokomo in the 1961 state final, may have had something to do with this. As the season progressed, however, Hoosier fans had no need to concern themselves about the twins playing aggressive basketball. In fact, in the school's seventh outing against eventual national champs Loyola, Dick and Tom completely dominated the first half. IU came into that contest with a 3-3 record, while Loyola was undefeated in as many outings.

Behind the aggressive efforts of Dick and Tom, the Hoosiers led 44-42 at halftime. Unfortunately the twins had picked up four and three fouls respectively in the first half. Both fouled out in the second half and the Hoosiers fell 106-94. Loyola's coach, George Ireland, had nothing but praise for the Van Arsdales. "They made us look disorganized," he told the press. "Man oh man, those two buzz-sawed us from both sides of the lane right down the middle."

". . .And they're only going to get tougher," McCracken assured Hoosier fans."

As the twins approached their first Big Ten season, they'd already learned quite a few lessons about the difference between the high school and college game. "On defense we soon discovered that you cannot leave your man alone even for a second. Every opponent we played had good quickness and if you took your eye off of them, they'd head right for the basket," reflects Tom. "We had to learn to be better shooters and deal with the problem of getting shots up against bigger and more physical players."

College basketball was also a lot more physical than the high school game. In a stretch of three games, Dick had the top of his head cut open, stitched up and then reopened two games later. This was quite a bit different from their high school days when only a few players were as tall and as physical. In addition to adjusting to the higher level of competition, the twins had become the subject of great expectations. The press and Hoosier fans expected Dick and Tom to lead the team in rebounding (they did), and to carry substantial scoring averages.

"I don't think we felt the pressure as much as we felt the need to learn from everything that was happening on the court," explains Tom. "We loved the game and we wanted to perform to the best of our abilities. I was frustrated sometimes---especially when we didn't get the calls that some of the older players got. I guess that's one of the differences between being a sophomore and being a junior or senior. I don't think we ever felt that we could not compete with the better players. It was more a matter of feeling a little more comfortable out on the court."

By the time Indiana faced Michigan State in their Big Ten opener, Branch had scrapped his plan to play Dick at guard. He moved Dave Porter into the guard spot (to throw the ball in to Rayl) and put Dick and Tom at forward with Tom Bolyard at center. This lineup, which had lost 73-70 in an earlier contest against Notre Dame, buried the Spartans 96-84. Rayl tallied forty-four points and Dick garnered thirteen rebounds---seven more than any other player on the floor.

In the Hoosiers' next contest against Purdue, it was Tom's turn to shine. Clearing the boards with a vengeance, Tom grabbed fourteen rebounds and scored twelve points. The Hoosiers' 85-71 victory came against a Boilermaker club that had Mel Garland and Ron Hughes, two players who'd given the twins a lot of grief in high school.

After winning their first three Big Ten contests, Indiana fell into a three-game losing streak. They finally broke out of it against tall and talented Minnesota. The Gophers met Indiana at a time when the twins were finally coming into their own. Dick and Tom hammered Minnesota on the boards. Gopher coach, Johnny Kundia, could only shake his head after the 80-77 upset. "They were the difference," he told reporters in a post-game interview. "We should have had the best of it in rebounding because we are a lot taller. But those twins really hustled. They come at you from both sides and meet somewhere in the middle. They're extremely physical. I can't imagine how good they'll be by the time they graduate."

The Hoosiers continued to play solid basketball, coming into their final Big Ten contest against Ohio State in third place with an 8-5 record. Along the way they'd posted an impressive victory against Michigan. A similar upset against Ohio State would give them and their fans a great deal of satisfaction.

The contest, played in the Fieldhouse at Indiana, was close from the opening tip to the final shot and was marred by a near riot which took place in the waning seconds when Rayl was knocked to the floor by two Ohio State players after accepting an inbounds pass.

Gary Bradds, the Buckeyes' All-American center

Dick goes up for a layup in Regional action versus Plainfield.

(Photo by Frank H. Fisse. Courtesy of Indianapolis Star)

Tom fouled by Bill Harte during Sectional play, 1961.

(Photo by Bob Daugherty. Courtesy of Indianapolis Star)

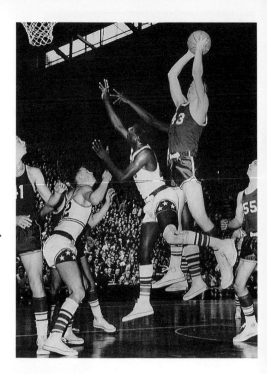

Tom battles Tell City's Tom Kron for a rebound in the afternoon of the 1961 State Final.

(Photo by Bob Daugherty. Courtesy of Indianapolis Star)

Tom soars for a rebound in State Tourney play, 1961.

(Photo by Frank Fisse. Courtesy of Indianapolis Star)

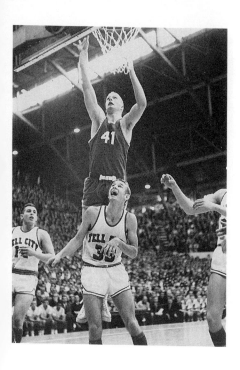

*Tom scores an
easy layup
versus Tell City!*

*(Photo by
Bob Daugherty.
Courtesy of
Indianapolis Star)*

*Dick fights Richie Scott
for a loose ball.
State Final, 1961.*

*(Photo Ed Lacey, Jr.
Courtesy of Indianapolis Star)*

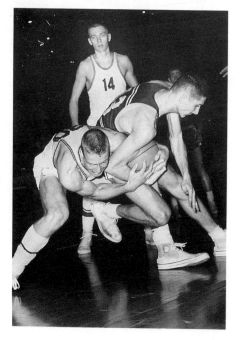

Tom elbows past Richie Scott at Kokomo in State Final action, 1961.

(Photo by Ed Lacey, Jr. Courtesy of Indianapolis Star)

Dick attempts a layup versus Detroit.
(Photo by Bob Gomel. Courtesy of Life Magazine)

Dick grabs a rebound versus Iowa.

(Photo courtesy of Dick Van Arsdale.)

Tom in an I.U. Intrasquad game.

(Photo by Frank H Fisse. Courtesy Indianapolis Star)

Dick chases a loose ball versus Missouri.
Tom (in background) looks on.
(Photo by Bob Gomel. Courtesy of Life Magazine)

From left to right: Hilda, Tom, Dick, and Raymond Van Arsdale, and Branch McCracken.

(Photo by Bob Gomel. Courtesy of Life Magazine)

Dick and Tom battle each other in practice.
(Photo by Bob Gomel. Courtesy of Life Magazine)

scored thirty-two points, but displayed poor judgement when he lost his temper and tried to take a swing at Rayl's head. When the two teams were not on the verge of a fight they played entertaining basketball. The score was 79-79 at the end of regulation and Indiana led 86-85 with only nine seconds left in overtime when Rayl was abused by two OSU players.

Hoosier fans, ecstatic about upsetting the first-place Buckeyes and angry over the treatment given to their star player, stormed the court and threatened to turn the event into a riot. When order was finally restored, Rayl hit one of his two free throws, giving the Hoosiers an 87-85 advantage. Ohio State could not score in the final seconds, losing for only the third time in Big Ten play. The loss threw them into a tie for first place with Illinois, sending Illinois to the national tournament (by virtue of the fact that Ohio State had gone to the tournament the previous year).

"This was our national championship game," McCracken told Jim Smith of the Indianapolis Times. "Our kids were tremendous. We out-hustled them and knocked them right out of the NCAA's." Tom Bolyard, who would later be named the team's most valuable player, scored twenty-nine points. Tom Van Arsdale hit eighteen and Dick grabbed twelve rebounds. The victory was a fitting finish to what had been a difficult season. Indiana ended the year with a 9-5 record in the Big Ten and 13-11 overall.

The twins' statistics in their first year of college basketball were almost identical: Tom scored 299 points, Dick totaled 292; Tom grabbed 223 rebounds, Dick pulled down 213; and Tom had 90 fouls while Dick was whistled for 82.

* *

During the Van Arsdales' junior season, the Hoosiers suffered through one of their worst campaigns in McCracken's tenure as head coach. The team had lost Rayl and Bolyard to graduation. They would sorely miss Jimmy's twenty-plus points per game and Bolyard's steady leadership and inside play. The 1963-64 Hoosiers did not have any seniors on scholarship. McCracken would start five juniors: Steve Redenbaugh and Al Harden at guard, Dick and Tom at forward, and 6'5" Jon McGlocklin at center.

In eleven warm-up contests for the Big Ten season, Indiana won six and lost five. Despite the relatively poor record, the Hoosiers' box scores began to show a fulfillment of the promises regarding Dick and Tom. They scored and rebounded well. Unfortunately, the rest of the team was not as spectacular. McGlocklin, almost always smaller than the opponent's center, had some great games, but was just too small to handle the better big men in college basketball. Redenbaugh and Harden were more than adequate as playmakers, but, understandably, lacked the scoring punch previously provided by Rayl.

Indiana lost its first five Big Ten contests and did not get out of the conference's cellar until their tenth game. A 93-72 victory against Purdue gave them a 3-7 record and put them one game up on Wisconsin.

The Hoosiers split their last four Big Ten contests and ended the season with an abysmal 9-15 record (5-9 in the Big Ten). Despite the team's poor showing, the Van Arsdales did quite well. They were named co-MVPs and also made honorable mention on UPI's All-American team. Dick, who had raised his grade point average to a B+, was also named to the Academic All- American team.

Maintaining a pace similar to their sophomore season

the twins were nearly equal in the key statistical categories after two years of play: Dick had garnered 535 points (22.3 per game) and grabbed 298 rebounds, while scored Tom 512 points (21.3 per game) and collected 295 rebounds.

* *

While much of Dick and Tom's time was devoted to playing basketball, they found time for a variety of other activities. Both were active in campus affairs and frequently spoke at social functions all around the state. "One of the greatest things about those twins was that they were not only good basketball players, they were also thoughtful, articulate young men who realized that others were looking at them as examples," recalls Lou Watson. "They were always aware of their responsibilities to the University and to their fans. No one had to tell them that they should be out promoting Indiana University. They did it on their own. I think it was this quality that has helped them become as successful as they are today."

Dick and Tom did well in the classroom. They were both named to the All-Big Ten Academic team and to the First Team Academic All-American squad. Tom was president of the "I" Men's Club, which is the organization for letter winners at Indiana University. The twins also participated in many of the fraternity social functions where Tom would usually escort one of many attractive young females he dated, while Dick would almost always arrive with Barbara Fenton, to whom he has now been married for over twenty-five years.

"Tom and I were always interested in girls," Dick explains. "In high school we'd been shy, but when we got to college we were able to get over some of that shyness and we both started dating right away. In fact, during our freshman orientation we both saw this girl, Janie

Lear. Tom and I both decided that we were going to call her and ask for a date. We argued about who was going to call her, but in the end neither one of us did.

"Not long after that, we were sitting in the Student Union and noticed two girls, Marty Berry and Barbara Fenton, at another table. We struck up a conversation with them. Barb did most of the talking, but I was more interested in Marty Berry at the time. Several weeks later, Fred Cook, one of our fraternity brothers, asked me if I could help him out of a jam. He was supposed to go out with Barb, but his girlfriend from home was going to be in Bloomington for the weekend. He hoped I would take her out to get him off the hook. Well, that was the best favor anyone has ever done for me. By the end of that first date, I felt quite comfortable with Barb. She was pretty and had a wonderful personality. It wasn't long before she and I were seeing a lot of each other."

"Dick met Barb during their freshman year and they've been together ever since, but Tom was different," says Jon McGlocklin. "He was with a different girl about every time I saw him. He always seemed to find the prettiest dates," says Jon McGlocklin. "We used to try and guess who he'd end up taking to the various parties. He once escorted Donna McKinley, an `Indianapolis 500' festival queen, and he used to be seen a lot with Jeannie Carol who was Miss Cheerleader USA."

During their years at IU, McGlocklin, Tom and Dick were almost always together. "It got to the point where guys in the fraternity were calling him the third twin,' laughs Tom, "but not to his face. Dick and I liked Jon right from the start. He had a great sense of humor and he could take an awful lot of ribbing."

"It's a good thing he could because if you planned on hanging around us, you could expect to have a joke or two pulled on you. Jon's dad was a character, too," adds Dick. "Zion McGlocklin was as big as a house and he had the reputation of being a bit of a hot-head. Zion came to most of our games and I believe he was every bit as proud of Jon as our parents were of us---but our parents were not quite as demonstrative as Zion. Once in a game against Purdue, a couple of Boilermakers had knocked Jon to the floor and he started a little fight with them. No sooner had the fight begun when Zion came lumbering out of the stands to help his son. Zion stumbled before he got out on the floor, but I don't think anyone who was there will ever forget the day ol' Zion was going to mix it up with those players from Purdue."

"Back in those days, people used to say I drank too much," says Zion, explaining his behavior. "I didn't drink at all. I was emotionally drunk. I don't remember the exact circumstances. Indiana was probably losing and a couple of those Boilermakers were giving my boy a rough time. Back then that was enough to get me riled up. I was sitting only two rows from the floor, but as I started climbing down I tripped over the trainer's box. All I remember was hearing Branch saying: `Where's Zion? Where's Zion?'

"Those were fun times. Indiana University basketball was like one big happy family. My wife and I were good friends with Mr. and Mrs. Van Arsdale and with the parents of the other boys. Branch was a great coach and a nice human being. He always made us feel comfortable. I'll tell you, with my boy and those twins Indiana was one of the toughest outfits going. If the team had only had a big man I believe they could have won it all."

* *

In their senior season, the Van Arsdales, McGlocklin, and the rest of the team came awfully close to earning a chance at winning it all. The Hoosiers came into that year with a lot more experience than the previous season, but the new year had not brought a solution to their dilemma in the middle.

The 1964-65 season also marked the end of the Branch McCracken era, as he would retire at the end of the season. Branch's players were determined to send him out a winner. McCracken, who had once written a book about basketball strategy, looked at the material with which he had to work and decided to make a drastic change in the Hoosiers' approach. Branch decided that his team would focus on defense---and he planned to have them pressure opponents from one end of the court to the other.

Branch devised a zone press that started whenever the opponent took the ball out of bounds under Indiana's basket. He developed a 2-2-1 full court zone where Dick and Tom were to position themselves near the end line. Their job was to put pressure on the person who received the inbounds pass. Jon McGlocklin, playing his senior season at his natural position, guard, and Steve Redenbaugh would position themselves about twenty feet behind the twins, and had the responsibility of patrolling the passing lanes. Center Ron Peyser protected from the center stripe back. The principle behind the zone was to double-team the man with the ball, hurrying him into making an error. While two players worked the double-team, the other three protected the passing lanes by continuously positioning themselves between the double-teamed man and the other players.

McCracken got the idea for this press from John Wooden, who was then coaching at UCLA. Wooden's Bruins had won a national championship without a player over 6'5".

"Last year we lost too many games by just a few

points---and we led most of those games at halftime," McCracken explained in his annual press conference. "Our problem came from the pressure of trying to defend our basket against taller players when our kids were getting tired. This year we hope our zone will put the pressure back on our opponents. A big man is a lot less effective at mid-court as opposed to under the basket." McCracken went on to explain that his deeper bench and more experienced squad would be able to handle the demands of playing defense from one end of the court to the other and of scoring lots of points.

The twins were excited about the zone defense, but realized that in playing such a high energy game they would probably not be on the floor as much as they'd been in previous seasons. The new system would require them to be unselfish, as more of the responsibility to score would be shifted to other players.

In addition to the changes demanded by a new philosophy on defense, the Van Arsdales were in their final year at Indiana and they could not resist speculating a bit about their futures. "We were both concerned about having a good year," Dick admits. "We certainly wanted to see our team do better than we had when we were juniors. We'd missed being picked to join the Olympic tryouts and many people thought one of the reasons we had not been chosen was because of our team's poor record. We were looking at the NBA draft at the end of the season and we didn't want to give those professional basketball teams any reason not to pick us. So I guess you could say we were about as focused on the coming season as two players could be."

With the twins determined to have a good season and Branch's 2-2-1 zone press, the Hoosiers were undefeated in their first nine outings prior to the Big Ten season.

Along the way they blasted Notre Dame (107-81), and made a shambles of St. Louis (98-68) and Memphis State (91-68) in winning Memphis State's version of a "Classic" holiday tournament. The thirty-point victory against St. Louis was especially rewarding. The Billikens had entered the holiday tournament with a #9 ranking in the polls.

Sporting a 9-0 record and ranked #2 in the nation, Indiana opened its Big Ten season against Illinois. The Illini pulled a joke on the pollsters, upsetting the highly-rated Hoosiers 86-81. Dick and Tom had a terrible night. Their combined shooting from the floor was an abysmal 11 for 34. "I'll never forget waking up the next morning and looking at the paper," recalls Al Harden, a guard on the 64-65 team. "We were ranked #2 in the country and we were in last place in the Big Ten."

That opening loss shocked Hoosier fans. In 1965 only the team that won the Big Ten could go to the NCAA tournament. And, while one loss certainly did not mean Indiana was out of the running, it did mean that they could hardly afford to lose another game.

Indiana won its next three games, but then did the unthinkable. They dropped a close one at home against Iowa (74- 68). McCracken was incensed after that game---not so much at his players as he was at State Fire Marshall Ira Anderson. Only days prior to the contest with Iowa, University trustees had reduced the Fieldhouse's capacity from 10,488 to 3,400 on Anderson's recommendation. The State Fire Marshall did not believe the Fieldhouse had enough exits for the larger crowd in the event of a fire.

"How in the world can these kids be expected to play basketball when the campus is in an uproar over this ticket thing?" Branch growled at the press in the post-game interview. "Ever since this attendance thing came up people have been driving my players nuts trying to get tickets.

"On top of that, playing in front of 3,400 people is like playing on a neutral court. When we played at Iowa we had 13,000 Hawkeye fans breathing down our neck. They come to our place and we've only got 3,400. Why didn't they do something about this exit thing months ago?"

While Branch was frustrated about the attendance "thing," his team had also suffered from the loss of Jon McGlocklin, who had hurt his ankle in the waning minutes of the Ohio State game. Fortunately, McGlocklin missed only one game and the situation at the Fieldhouse was corrected before the Hoosiers' next home contest.

The Hoosiers quickly got back on the right track and ran their conference record to 5-2. They felt they still had a chance at winning the Big Ten, but they would need to win the rest of their games to do it---and winning the rest of their games would require beating undefeated Michigan. Michigan, rated the best team in the nation in some polls, featured Cazzie Russell, Oliver Darden, Bill Buntin, and Larry Tregoning. They'd waltzed through their Big Ten season without a loss and came into IU's fieldhouse with all of the swagger associated with the better teams in the land.

Indiana, too, brought plenty of confidence into this contest. The Hoosiers had run off impressive victories in their games after the Iowa loss. The Van Arsdales and McGlocklin were at least the equal of Michigan's scoring trio---and Indiana would have the lungs of ten thousand fans to support them.

The game carried all of the advance hoopla of a major sporting event. Reporters from around the country crowded the press box, while dozens of radio and television station employees jockeyed for broadcast positions on either side of the scorer's table. On the floor, the Hoosiers and Wolverines delivered scintillating performances. They gave everyone who watched or listened a game to remember.

After thirty-eight minutes and fifty-one seconds of play Indiana proved to be the better of the two. They led by seven points (81-74). In the last sixty-nine seconds, however, Michigan, behind an outstanding performance from junior sensation Cazzie Russell, scored seven unanswered points and forced the game into overtime.

In the overtime, Indiana used the first three minutes fashioning a 92-88 advantage---but then spent the remaining two minutes squandering scoring opportunities and wasting their four- point lead. Michigan pulled back into a tie as Larry Tregoning hit two free throws and Bill Buntin, the Wolverines' fabulous senior center, tipped in a Cazzie Russell's errant jump shot to force a second overtime.

Michigan scored the first two points in the second overtime, but Indiana again managed to pull ahead (95-94) with fifty-five seconds remaining. Unfortunately, not more than twenty seconds later Tom committed his fifth foul. As the second twin took a seat on the bench (Dick had fouled out in regulation), Russell hit both free throws, putting the Wolverines on top 96-95 with only twenty-six seconds on the clock.

The Hoosiers, desperately in need of another bucket quickly solved Michigan's press---but no sooner had they crossed the ten second line when Jon McGlocklin was whistled for a charging foul. And even then all hope was not lost---Bill Buntin travelled, giving the ball back to Indiana. The Hoosiers' last shot was taken by Steve Redenbaugh who attempted a lean-in jumper from inside the key. Bill Buntin redeemed himself by blocking it. The final claxon blared on a 96-95 Michigan victory.

The aftermath of the contest was pure bedlam. Lou Watson nearly came to blows with Michigan's coach Dave Strack and McCracken was so incensed at his players that he "chewed out" his team in the locker room after the game.

"My God, boys, you sure let one get away tonight," McCracken roared in front of a locker room full of reporters. Visibly shaken, Branch railed against a litany of Hoosier errors. He complained about his team's free throw shooting (they missed fifteen), their sloppy passing, and untimely shooting. "We had them. We had them cold and we let them get away," he whispered shaking his head and then perked up a bit and added: "But keep you chins up, hold your heads high. You're a good ball club. Forget about practice tomorrow and think this one over in your own minds."

The thoughts stirring in Dick and Tom's mind involved the loss of their fourth big game in a row. In high school it had been Southport, Tech, and Kokomo and now, in a big college game, another loss at the wire. In all four contests either one or the other or both had watched their team fail in the waning seconds while sitting on the bench saddled with five fouls. "I guess if anybody wanted to start pointing fingers they'd just as well begin with us," says Tom, who lead the Hoosiers in both scoring (27) and rebounds (11). "Neither one of us were around at the end. It is hard to describe the frustration. I don't think either one of us could have tried any harder or wanted that victory any more. We always hated to lose and we took the loss against Michigan especially hard. The only game we'd ever played that had more riding on the line was the one we'd lost to Kokomo."

"...But tomorrow always comes," Dick interjects. "Our philosophy has always been that if you give one hundred percent today you'll have few regrets tomorrow. Those big losses hurt like hell, but we can't go back and change the final score. We had to take whatever lessons we could learn from the experience and move on."

Stunned by the defeat at the hands of the Wolverines, Indiana lost two more Big Ten contests and ended the conference schedule with a 9-5 record.

Prior to the end of the season, Branch McCracken announced his retirement from coaching. The team and its fans bid him goodbye during a home game against Purdue. His team sent him out a winner, posting a 90-79 victory. "It was great to send him out a winner," Tom smiles. "Branch was a great coach and a fabulous person. He wanted us to believe that we could win any game we played no matter the odds. As a coach he was a powerful motivator. He gave the greatest locker room talks and he was a fine public speaker as well."

"But we also remember him as a good person," Dick adds. "Branch treated us all as though we were his own kids. Once when Tom and I came down with the flu, we were laid up in our dorm feeling miserable and Branch came by with soup and orange juice. He sat there and visited with us for awhile and by the time he left we both felt a little better. Branch was a great guy. I enjoyed playing for him. We wish we could have won another national championship for him, but that was not possible. Even so, we were glad to send him out a winner."

When the curtain closed on the twins' senior season they busied themselves with their last semester of school while eagerly anticipating the NBA's draft which would take place in May. Dick and Tom closed out their college careers with remarkably similar statistics: Dick scored

1240 points and grabbed 719 rebounds; Tom scored 1252 points and cornered 719 rebounds. In their senior year, both were chosen as forwards on the All Big Ten team and both were members of the Academic All-American basketball team, as well as being named to numerous other All-American teams.

Tom pursues a loose ball versus Missouri.
Photo by Bob Gamel courtesy Life Magazine

Tom fires up a shot against Detroit while Dick positions himself for a rebound. Photo by Bob Gamel courtesy Life Magazine.

Chapter 5

NBA rookies Dick for the Knicks and Tom for the Pistons.
Photos (left) Albert Barg (right) George Kalinsky

With college behind them, Dick and Tom prepared for their entrance into the National Basketball Association. The NBA they were about to join was different from the NBA today. In 1965 professional basketball did not draw nearly as many fans and, to keep costs down and attendance up, doubleheaders were not uncommon. The league had only nine teams, which were divided into two divisions, creating strong rivalries between the franchises. The star players did not even come close to making what bench warmers make today. And, while the NBA was on relatively solid financial footing, the league had only recently been able to say with any certainty that it would be around for a long time. Even so, in 1965 the National Basketball Association represented the most successful venture into professional basketball.

The pro game has been around almost from the time basketball was invented by Dr. Naismith in 1891. Most experts agree that the first bona fide professional game was played in 1896 at a Masonic Temple in Trenton, New Jersey. Participants made about fifteen dollars each for their performance.

Professional basketball was born out of amateur leagues, which played in YMCAs all along the eastern seaboard. The Ys, however, were forced to ban the better teams as many of the participants played too rough, causing numerous fights. The Ys closed their doors to these "serious" basketball players, forcing them to rent dance halls for their games. In order to pay the rent (and pay the doctor's bills) teams had to charge admission.

The first league, called the National Basketbal League, was formed in 1902, but lasted only one season Throughout the early 1900s several professiona basketball leagues briefly flourished and then floundered

Following the tradition laid down by the firs

professional teams, leagues such as the NBL did not play their games in gymnasiums. They generally played in dance halls on 60'x40' dance floors, encircled by chicken wire (which led to the coining of the term "cagers"). These floors were slick with wax, which impeded players from making any kind of a quick move. Thus, the sport was not even close to being as exciting as it is today.

In those early years, spectators could usually expect to be entertained by the violent nature of the game's participants. Contests were quite physical. Many games had to be suspended when fights broke out and the police were called in.

Among the best known players from this first era of professional basketball were Joe Lapchick and Nat Holman. They played for a team called "The Original Celtics." Other great teams included an African-American outfit from Harlem "The Renaissance Big Five." The "Rens," as they were called in the papers, had an amazing run of 147 victories against only seven defeats.

Unfortunately, by the time World War II came around, basketball had still not caught on as a professional sport. Games were boring (aside from the fights) and poorly attended. After the war, however, several concerted efforts were made to make the professional game as entertaining as the college game, which, after the elimination of the center jump after every basket and the "ten second rule," was quickly becoming a favorite of winter fans. Individuals such as Maurice Podoloff, the first commissioner of the NBA, believed that outlawing zone defenses and encouraging more offense would make professional basketball much more pleasing to watch.

Incorporating these principles, the National Basketball Association was born in 1949. A consolidation of the National Basketball League (NBL) and the

Basketball Association of America (BAA), the league started its first season with seventeen teams.

Sixteen years later the league was down to nine clubs: New York, Philadelphia, Detroit, Boston, Baltimore, San Francisco, Los Angeles, St. Louis, and Cincinnati. Many of the original franchises had been in small midwestern towns such as Tri-Cities, Fort Wayne, and Sheybogan, and by 1960, all of those small town teams, save for Rochester and Syracuse, had folded. By the time Dick and Tom entered the NBA, Rochester and Syracuse were gone as well.

* *

The cream of the talent pool available for the 1965 National Basketball Association draft included such stars as Rick Barry (Miami), Bill Bradley (Princeton), Billy Cunningham (North Carolina), Jerry Sloan (Evansville), and Gail Goodrich (UCLA). Selected twelfth (Dick) and thirteenth (Tom), the Van Arsdales were second round picks of New York and Detroit, respectively.

Following the lead of professional football, the NBA built its success on the shoulders of great college players. George Mikan, Dolph Schayes, Bob Pettit, and Bob Cousy were among the game's earliest stars. They were followed by the first round of pro basketball's superstars such as Wilt Chamberlain, Oscar Robertson, Jerry West, Bill Russell, and Elgin Baylor.

Dick and Tom's graduating class added Bill Bradley, Rick Barry, and Billy Cunningham to the ranks of the league's better players. Other great players of their era included Willis Reed, Dave DeBusschare, Dave Bing, Jerry Lucas, Walt Frazier, Earl "The Pearl" Monroe, and John Havlicek.

During the twins' early years in the NBA, the nine teams kept only ten players. Therefore, being a member of a professional basketball team implied that you were among the ninety best players in the world.

". . .And you had to play your butt off every night to keep your spot on the roster," recalls Rick Barry, who was the first player chosen in the '65 draft.

"There weren't any easy games," adds Tom. "Can you imagine having to play against Wilt or Bill Russell nine times each season? We had to play against great competition every night and, generally speaking, there was no such thing as a `home court advantage.' The league was still struggling for attendance so we played a lot of home games in places away from home. We went wherever the team owner figured we could draw a crowd."

"People have this idea that professional athletes have always made great money," says Dick. "But this is not true. When Tom and I signed our first professional contracts, neither one of us made over fifteen thousand dollars. (For the sake of comparison, an MBA made eight to ten thousand in 1965.) We planned to work during the off-season just to make ends meet.

"When we came into the league, we had no idea how much the pay would increase over the years. Our primary interest was just being able to continue to play basketball for a few more years.

"In fact, Bill Bradley, the Knicks' first pick that year, had a Rhodes scholarship to Oxford College in England. He went to Oxford instead of immediately signing with the Knicks. I cannot imagine a player of Bill's caliber doing the same thing today."

"I honestly thought the World University Games would be my last stint as a basketball player," remarks Bradley. "And when I did decide to play professional basketball, I made the decision because I loved the game. There were very few of us in a position to look at pro ball as a career.

Those of us who played during that particular era did it because we loved the game."

"In the event that we would not be able to play professional ball, Tom and I had both taken the entrance exam for law school and had been accepted to IU's school of law," Dick explains. But after being drafted by the Knicks, I never really gave continuing my education a second thought. My goal for as long as I can remember had been to be the member of a professional basketball team. I would not have passed that up for anything. On the other hand, I did expect to be paid. Some guys say they would play for nothing. I would not have played for nothing."

* *

The NBA draft represented the fruition of Dick and Tom's lifelong ambition, but it also marked the end of their lives together. "We'd talked about that, too," Dick explains. "We knew people were looking at us and wondering how we would respond on our own. I think we tried to convince each other that it was important to continue all the things that had brought us success. We were both determined not to fail---but it was hard to move on. Our years together had been fabulous and it was difficult to imagine what life would be like without Tom beside me. There's no doubt it was going to be a tremendous adjustment.

"One thing that helped me adjust was the fact that Barb and I were becoming closer. Even though she and I, too, were going to be apart for awhile (Barb took a teaching position in Chicago during Dick's first year with the Knicks), I think my relationship with her helped me to catch a glimpse of what my future could be like.

"I remember thinking that I definitely had more hard work in front of me, and I realized I was just going to have to make the best of the situation and hope that by some miracle Tom and I would end up on the same team again."

While Dick managed to face this adjustment without too much difficulty, the situation threw Tom into a quandary. "I must admit that in some ways draft day was the worst day of my life. I didn't know what to do. I wanted to play basketball, but I was disturbed by the notion of having to be alone. I don't know what I'd been thinking. I guess I had hoped that Dick and I would be picked by the same team, but I didn't really believe that would happen. I suppose I just blocked those thoughts out of my mind and when the situation was staring me in the face I reacted out of desperation or something."

Tom signed his contract and went to training camp, but then left camp and came home. "One night I turned to Rod Thorn who was my roommate at training camp and said: `If I'm not here in the morning, let Debusschere know that I quit and went home.' I got up early the next morning and headed for Bloomington to buy my textbooks for law school."

"He said he'd changed his mind and decided he ought to go to law school," recalls his mother. "I would have been happy to see him go to law school, but I knew right away that he was having trouble dealing with being apart. I really didn't know what I could do. I'd always thought he wanted to play basketball a heck-of-a-lot more than he wanted to go back to school."

Dick also realized that his brother was about to give up something they had both worked twelve years to get. "When he called and told me what he'd done, I reminded him that his dream had always been to be a professional basketball player. I told him that if he quit now he'd regret it for the rest of his life, and he'd better get his ass back to Detroit or I was going to be extremely mad. What else could I tell him?"

"I went back to camp and Dave Debusschere (Detroit's player/coach) told me he'd take me back, but that I was done if it happened again. Eventually, I made the adjustment and, looking back, I think we both agree that being separated was definitely in our best interest. In the long run it helped both of us."

* *

During their first NBA season, the twins proved to be steady, if not spectacular, performers. By the season's end, both had earned starting spots on their respective teams. Dick averaged twelve points per game at forward for the Knicks while Tom scored an average of ten points per contest for Detroit. The twins were both named to the league's first team all-rookie squad. "I think professional basketball suited our games even better than college ball," Tom explains. "We were both physical players, and in the NBA you had to be as physical as you could be."

"It seemed that each higher level required me to be willing to take more physical abuse and to dish it out," adds Dick. "I also believe that the NBA we played in was definitely as physical as it is today."

"Of course Dick says that," laughs Rick Barry. "He dished that stuff out as well as he took it. He and I had some battles; in fact, one night in Baltimore we nearly came to blows. With guys like him and his brother around you had to expect to be run over and wrestled every night out. If the NBA was rough, it was because guys like Dick and Tom made it that way."

In addition to the physical play, or on account of it, Dick and Tom both discovered that they needed to work harder at becoming better shooters. "I'd say we were adequate shooters coming out of college," Tom assesses.

"But during the summer when we travelled to Europe as a part of the World University team, we both saw that we were going to have to do a better job of hitting the outside shot. Bill Bradley, who was a member of that team, showed us a few things that really helped us learn to be better shooters."

"The trip to Europe did a lot for our confidence, too," maintains Dick. "It was the first time we played on a championship caliber team where most of our teammates were as good or better than us. Lou Hudson, Billy Cunningham, Bill Bradley, Joe Ellis, and Fred Hetzel were on the team. By playing and practicing with those guys, we learned a few things that certainly helped us as pros. Being a part of the World University Games was also a great way to cap off our college education. Spending time in the countries where we played was an education in and of itself. When we were in France, for example, Bill Bradley, Tom, and I made a rule that we had to speak in French the whole time we were there. We should have known better than to make such a deal with Bill. He was practically fluent in French while Tom and I struggled with it like a couple of tourists."

"I remember that," laughs Senator Bradley. "They weren't so bad at French. We had a great time during that trip. I roomed with Tom and he, Dick and I got along well right from the start. I enjoyed getting to know them while we were in Europe and our friendship continued when I came to New York to play for the Knicks.

"As basketball players they were remarkably similar. I remember being most impressed with their tenacious practice habits. Those two would go full out every time they were on the court. Especially when they were guarding each other. I don't believe I've ever seen two players go at each other as hard as they did. As I recall, I did give them a pointer or two about shooting, but they taught me some things about defense and intensity, too."

If professional basketball required the twins to make changes in the way they played, it also required them to make adjustments off the court as well. One adjustment was growing accustomed to the grueling schedule. "In college we played three games in one week once or twice during the entire season. We played some games back-to-back, too. But professional basketball required us to play at least three times a week and back-to-back games were common," Dick explains. "When you combine that playing schedule with all of those late night or early morning flights and bus rides, in addition to a rigorous pre-season camp and the numerous practices and team meetings during the season--- basketball became an all-consuming occupation."

"And you couldn't just go through the motions," adds Tom. "We were being paid to play and there's nothing a sports fan (or journalist) will pick-up on more quickly than a guy who's being paid to play sports and is just going through the motions. Of course, there were going to be tough nights; nights when you didn't feel well or were just plain tired. But even then you had to tough it out and try to do your best. The last thing I wanted the paying customers to think was that I wasn't doing everything I could to help my team win.

"Everybody has things in their life that are hard for them to do," Dick interjects. "And even if the travelling was tough and the schedule hectic---I was doing what I wanted to be doing. I had achieved my goal. It would have been extremely ungrateful of me to give anything less than my best."

Dick also faced an adjustment in moving from the Midwest to New York. "I didn't give that much thought," says Dick. "New York was certainly a lot bigger than any city I'd ever seen, but it wasn't all that intimidating. The Knicks provided single players with rent-free housing in the Paramount Hotel, which was within walking distance of Madison Square Garden where we practiced and played our home games. So I didn't have to worry about getting lost or finding a place to live.

"The Paramount wasn't the classiest hotel in town, but it was all right for me. The only thing about the hotel that I really remember is the pigeons. I got to know the pigeons pretty well. They'd wake me up every morning, and my room, for reasons I cannot explain, always had feathers in it. Aside from that and an occasional flood from the room above me, the hotel was just fine."

Tom took up residence at the Lafayette Plasiance in downtown Detroit where he roomed with veteran Don Kojis (Marquette) and Ron Reed who had played ball for Notre Dame and would later play major league baseball. "That first year is a blur to me," Tom admits. "Ron, Don, and I spent a lot of time together. We were out of town for weeks at a time during the season. In fact, we were in New York at least ten times. We took part in doubleheaders and then after the games the players from all four teams would generally go out to the same places. I got to know many of the guys from around the league.

"The other thing that stands out in my mind was all the times we had to go up against great talent. We played Boston nine times every year. I hated seeing Bill Russell that many times. In college we saw a few great players, but only now and then. In the NBA we competed against great players every night.

"The competition was difficult, but at the same time it was exciting. I'll never forget the first time I went head-to-head against Oscar Robertson. Oscar had played high school basketball in Indianapolis and many of my earliest basketball memories involve some the incredible things he did as a high school player. In fact, when Dick and I were in grade school we saw him at a track meet once and we even asked him for his autograph.

"The first time I played against him was in an exhibition game in Indianapolis. My parents, aunts, uncles, grandparents, high school classmates---everyone I knew showed up for that game. Of course, I knew they'd come to see me so I was pumped up and wanted to do a good job. I scored twenty-four points and my name was all over the morning papers."

Perhaps the most unique event of Dick and Tom's first professional season happened during the very first game. The New York Knicks opened at home against the Detroit Pistons and, for the first time in their playing careers, Dick and Tom faced each other as opponents on the basketball court.

In the first of many head-to-head confrontations, Dick's team won 111-103, but Tom out scored his brother nine points to four. "I didn't like guarding him, but it seemed like every time we played against each other my coach wanted me to guard Tom and his coach would have Tom guarding me," Dick ruefully recalls.

"I guess what bothered me most was that I always wanted to see Dick do well. If I was guarding him, I had to take a different attitude," explains Tom. "When playing against Dick, I also had to switch from forward to guard. I had some good games against him and he against me, but in all the times we played against each other, I seldom got into as good a groove as I did in other games."

Both twins describe their first season as a blur of activity. "I don't remember much about any particular game," Dick offers. "But I do remember thinking that I had to play against a tough opponent every night out. We played Tuesday night doubleheaders almost every week. I met a lot of the other players in the league at those doubleheaders and we used to go out after the games. I think we socialized between teams a lot more than they do today.

"We played a doubleheader on New Year's Eve during my rookie year. I remember Jon McGlocklin (who played for the Cincinnati Royals at that time) and I went out after the games and we happened to end up in the same restaurant with Wilt Chamberlain. Wilt was just about the most famous basketball player alive at that time and, while we knew him and he knew us, it wasn't as though we rookies would feel comfortable enough to go over and start `chewing the fat' with him. Anyway, Wilt was in a generous mood that night---he sent a bottle of champagne over to our table. I guess that was his way of saying: `Welcome to the big leagues.'"

When their first pro season came to a conclusion, Dick and Tom were both confident that they could indeed compete in the NBA. And again, as had been the case throughout their careers, both of them looked beyond their personal accomplishments, setting their sights on winning a championship---a world championship.

As they packed their bags and headed for home, however, this possibility seemed remote. In New York, Dick played for two different head coaches (Harry Gallatin and Dick Mcguire) and the team finished last. Tom played for player/coach Dave DeBusschere. Unfortunately, DeBusschere could not inspire his team to anything better than a fifth place finish in a five team division.

* *

While the twins were quickly establishing themselves as two of the emerging stars in the NBA, the country had begun to immerse itself into a "police action" in Vietnam. By the spring of 1966, thousands of young men were being drafted into the army and sent to Southeast Asia to fight an undeclared war. Dick and Tom were prime targets for this deadly draft.

The twins were as apolitical as two young men could be, and both disdained the idea that they would be asked to forego professional basketball careers in exchange for uniforms and a gun. Seeking a way to fulfill their obligation to their country while continuing to play professional basketball, they joined the Indiana Air National Guard.

As new members of the Guard, Dick and Tom spent six weeks of the summer after their first NBA season in the muggy barracks of a military base in Amarillo, Texas, receiving basic training. "I don't remember much about it except to say that those drill sergeants worked us harder than any coach I've ever had," Tom recalls. "Basic training was not a pleasant experience."

For the next six years, Dick and Tom had to come back to Terre Haute, Indiana for one weekend each month and for two weeks in the summer. "A lot of guys got sent to Vietnam and many of them did not come back, so it's inappropriate for us to complain. We came back to Indiana once a month for six years and then spent two weeks each summer in training," Dick asserts. "We were assigned to the National Guard camp at Hulman Field in Terre Haute so we'd fly to Indianapolis or Chicago and then drive to Terre Haute. Guard duty usually cost us five or six games each year, but we both realize it could have been worse."

"If we'd been about an inch taller, we would not have

had a problem," adds Tom. "The military did not accept people who were 6'6" or taller. The height restriction saved the NBA from losing as many players as baseball or football. Even so, we knew a number of guys who were in the same situation as us."

After finishing basic training, Dick followed through on plans he'd made in late 1965. He married Barbara Fenton.

"I guess you could say that after basic training I was ready for anything," Dick jokes and then adds. "We'd been dating for five years and I had known for a long time that I wanted to spend the rest of my life with her. But I didn't ask her earlier because I wanted to establish in my mind that I could play professional basketball and provide for a family.

"Early in my first year with the Knicks I came to the conclusion that I was good enough to compete in the NBA and I figured I would get a raise or two along the way so I gave Barb and engagement ring at Christmas. Marrying Barb is one of the smartest things I've ever done. We've had a wonderful life together."

"From the very beginning, ours was a different kind of relationship," explains Barb. "When Fred Cook fixed Dick and me up for a date I had no idea what to expect. Dick took me to a mid-term party at his fraternity house. It was called the `Tension Suspension.' The fraternity had this tradition where they'd toss old televisions, refrigerators, and so on from the windows of the fraternity house. It was a strange way to relieve tension, but it certainly made for an interesting first date.

"It wasn't always easy dating a basketball player at Indiana in those days either. Branch didn't like his players to be with girls so when Dick and I would walk together he'd duck into the bushes if he thought he saw

Branch coming.

"I wasn't a big fan of basketball, but I knew a little about the game because my father was a big fan. In fact, the first time I ever saw Dick and Tom was when they were accepting their Trester Award after the state final loss to Kokomo. My dad had the game on the TV and I caught a glimpse of them as I was headed out to do something.

"After I started dating Dick, I began to follow the game a little more closely, but when he was drafted by the New York Knicks in the NBA I had no idea what that meant. I do remember thinking it was great that Dick was going to be able to continue to play basketball, although I never really thought of it as a career.

"At IU Dick and Tom were two of the most popular guys on campus. I remember when the photographer from *Life* magazine followed them around for a week. When the magazine came out they received quite a few phone calls and letters from girls at other colleges around the country. They handled that pretty well, but knowing Dick and Tom as I did I could not resist pulling a little trick on them. I had a sorority sister call them on the phone and pretend that she was from a college in Texas. She told them that she and several of her sorority sisters were headed to Chicago for vacation and that they wanted to stop in Bloomington to see him and Tom.

"We had a date on the night these girls were supposed to visit so I was curious to see if Dick would break the date. Sure enough, we were not out for more than an hour when he mentioned that he had to go to a meeting. I suppose I should have been angry, but, even though he was doing something deceitful, I wasn't. In fact, I was kind of pleased to see that he wasn't perfect. I guess he and Tom and several of their fraternity brothers waited for those gals from Texas for quite awhile. When I confronted him about it, he became the most embarrassed young man I'd ever seen."

"Can you believe that sweet young girl would do such a mean thing? For the record, the only reason Tom and I went to the hotel was to introduce those girls from Texas to our fraternity brothers," Dick responds in jest. "I'm glad she has such a wonderful sense of humor, but I wasn't so nearly as amused as she was about that particular episode. But as I look back at our years at Indiana, I have many pleasant memories. I was quite fortunate to find a young woman as pleasant to be with as Barb. If my head was in the clouds, she'd get my feet back on the ground and if I was feeling down, she'd cheer me up.

"One of the big things in those days was for fraternity guys to give their girlfriends their fraternity pins. I guess it was like a pre-engagement. It was called `getting pinned.' Barb and I had been going together for several years and I still had not `pinned' her. I had not done this because Branch was opposed to such things and I didn't want to upset him. Then, during one of our last semesters, Barb made a sweater for me. It didn't fit and I really did not like it. I wanted to give it back to her, but I didn't want to make her mad so I pinned my fraternity pin to the sweater and then gave it back to her."

"I was so mad at him about returning the sweater I didn't even notice the pin until I was back in my room about to burst into tears," Barb laughs. "Dick had some strange ways of expressing himself back then. One time he sent me a jewelry box and when I opened it I found a petrified pig's heart and note that said: `Here's my heart.' He was a little strange, but I grew to like him.

"When he went to New York I went home to Chicago to

teach school. We had not talked much about marriage, but I think we both felt that one day soon we would be married. When I visited him at Christmas he gave me an engagement ring. Ironically, when I left New York I went to Cincinnati for Marty Berry's wedding. (She had been the girl whom Dick was admiring when he and Barb first met.)

"We were married the following August in Chicago and then packed all of our belongings into a U-Haul and drove to Long Island. We had to stop at a motel one night along the way and I didn't sleep a wink for fear that some one would steal the trailer full of our things while we slept.

"Our first home was an apartment in West Hempstead on Long Island. When we moved in I was able to get a teaching position at Franklin Square, which was not far from home.

"Those early years of marriage were fun. New York was a fascinating city and we enjoyed living there. When we were deciding where to live I was concerned about how I'd get around, but I never worried much about crime or any of the things you often hear about New York. We never had any problems. In fact, I used to take the Long Island subway into New York and then catch a cab to Madison Square Garden to see Dick play. I don't know if an unescorted girl could do that today.

"The Pistons played quite a few games at the Garden so we saw a lot of Tom, too. I enjoyed going to the games. Dick was doing well and the Knicks were getting better. made friends with some of the other players' wives and we'd often go out together after the games.

"In my own profession, teaching at Franklin Square was challenging and it kept me occupied during the Knicks' road trips. After the first year, I was pretty well settled and I hoped we'd be in New York for a long time."

Chapter 6

Tom Van Arsdale as a Cincinnati Royal.

By 1967 the NBA added three new teams: the Chicago Bulls, the San Diego Rockets and the Seattle Supersonics. In addition to Seattle, Chicago, and San Diego, the league, buoyed by four years of unprecedented growth in attendance, had plans for additional expansion over the next several seasons.

Among the reasons for the league's rise in prominence was the emergence of a dominating team the Boston Celtics. In a string of eight seasons, Boston had won eight consecutive championships. The Celtics' success made their coach Red Auerbach, and players Bill Russell, Bob Cousy, and K.C. Jones household names and brought extra attention to pro basketball--especially during the tournament. Wilt Chamberlain and the Philadelphia 76ers represented the Celtics' biggest rivalry. Chamberlain was one of those flamboyant athletes that fans either loved or hated and the Celtics were one of those teams that fans either loved or hated. Chamberlain's battles against the Celtics' quiet giant, Bill Russell, made playoff contests between the two teams a major sports attraction. Games between Boston and Philly were often televised as fans loved to watch the game's best two big men go at each other.

While the Celtics and Philadelphia generally dominated the Eastern Conference, New York and Baltimore were never far behind. Baltimore featured high-flying Gus Johnson, a forward whose flamboyant dunks had the fans oohing and aahing. In 1967 the Bullets added Earl "The Pearl" Monroe. Monroe's dribbling and passing would give Bullet (and later Knick) fans a thrill a minute. The Bullets would eventually acquire Wes Unseld, who would lead them to an NBA title. The New York Knicks featured Dick Van Arsdale Walt Bellamy, Willis Reed and Dick Barnett. Many observers believed that if the Knicks could finally sign Bill Bradley they would solve the puzzle that would make them contenders. In the summer of 1967, the Knicks not only signed Bradley, they also drafted a talented young guard named Walt Frazier.

Pro basketball was catching on in the Midwest as well. The Minneapolis Lakers with Jerry West and Elgin Baylor were the class of the league's Western Division. That franchise received a tremendous boost when it moved to Los Angeles and acquired Wilt Chamberlain from the world champion Philadelphia 76ers. Los Angelinos quickly fell in love with the Lakers and the team has become one of the most successful sports franchises in history. The St. Louis Hawks with aging Cliff Hagan, Richie Guerin and the youthful Lou Hudson were also among the best in the West. The team eventually left St. Louis, relocating in Atlanta.

San Francisco, anchored by veterans Al Attles and Nate Thurmond, had added a scoring machine named Rick Barry, which made them a definite contender. In Cincinnati Oscar Robertson, perhaps the greatest basketball player of any era, thrilled fans with his scoring, rebounding, and passing. Unfortunately, the Royals, who also featured former OSU great, Jerry Lucas, were unable to win the big games.

Tom's team, the Pistons, lacked a big man and had been beset with injury problems during his first two seasons. Yet attendance at Piston games continued to increase. In 1967 Detroit would look to rookie Dave Bing to give them a boost. Bing, coupled with former Purdue star Terry Dischinger and Dave Debusschere, figured to challenge the top two teams in the west.

Dick and Tom fit into their respective teams as the "fifth man." They were starting players who could be counted on to give steady performances night in and night out. Physically and mentally tough, Dick and Tom generally operated outside of the spotlight. They were required to play a lot of minutes and to provide their teams with whatever was needed, but they seldom made the headlines in the next day's paper.

"The Vans were a rare commodity in the NBA," recalls Cotton Fitzsimmons. "They could play guard or forward, they could score if they needed to score, or rebound, or bring the ball downcourt, and always played tough defense. You could count on Dick and Tom to play as many minutes as necessary and to give you all they had for all of those minutes."

"They weren't spectacular in the sense that they made amazing plays or excited the crowd with their skills," explains Billy Cunningham. "They just played their butts off. You almost had to be on the court with them to fully appreciate what they did. I'll never forget the first time I played against them. They were at IU and we came to their place for a game. Jimmy Rayl was playing then and he'd come down on a three-on-one break and put up a shot from the top of the key. He was spectacular. But Dick and Tom were steady and solid. They grabbed rebound after rebound and hit the shots when they were open or passed off when they were not.

"In the pros, I think Tom was a little better shooter from the outside and Dick would drive to the basket more. Other than that I think they both played the same way--- in your face for forty-eight minutes."

"There were guys playing professional basketball that had more talent than Dick and Tom," offers John Havlicek, "but I can't think of many who played the game any harder than they did. Dick and Tom are a classic example of what happens when someone wants something and works as hard as they can to get it."

* *

During the 1967-68 season both New York and Detroit made coaching changes. The Knicks hired Red Holtzman to replace Dick Mcguire. New York had brought Mcguire in to turn things around after the disastrous start in '65 under Gallatin, but Mcguire was not in the team's long-term plans as head coach. With the changes made during the previous season, including the signing of rookie sensation Walt Frazier and the return of Bill Bradley from England, management decided to bring in a new coach. Holtzman had been with the team for several seasons and one of his primary functions had been to teach rookies the art of defense in professional basketball. Thus, he was the natural choice for the younger, offensively stronger team.

"Red definitely stressed defense," Dick recalls. "One of his pet peeves was players who turned away from the ball when retreating on defense. During practices he'd stand on the sideline with a ball under his arm and, if you weren't watching the opponent bring the ball upcourt as you retreated on defense, he'd throw the ball he was holding at the back of your head.

"When I joined the Knicks in '65 he was instrumental in teaching me things like how to fight through a pick without being whistled for a foul, or how to make a jump switch without getting `backdoored.' Red was fiery coach and I enjoyed playing for him."

In Detroit Dave Debusschere had decided that he no longer wanted the dual responsibilities of coaching and playing. Debusschere resigned his coaching position and the Pistons brought in Donnis Butcher to replace him.

"I think Dave did everything he could to help us win," Tom offers. "He was a great team player and an excellent defender and shooter. Debusschere was young as far as coaches go, but he was mature for his age. Being a player/coach is difficult and if the team isn't winning the difficulties are magnified. In the end I think losing is what drove Dave out of coaching.

"Donnis Butcher, his replacement, had a wonderful, take-no- prisoners attitude. He had earned my respect even before he became head coach. Donnis was still playing when I joined the team and one day in practice I drove around him for a layup, sticking my left arm out to keep him away from me. Butcher came across the top of my arm with a vicious karate chop and then got right in my face and said: `Rookie if you ever do that to me again I'm going to break you in two.' He was a fighter. When he took over, one of the first rules he made was that anybody who stayed on the bench during a fight would be fined."

Butcher, assigned the task of turning one of the division's worst teams into a contender, faced an uphill struggle---a struggle that led him to make some changes---one of which was to trade Tom to Cincinnati.

"I liked playing for Donnis, but I did not play for him for very long," Tom recalls. "Thirty-seven games into my third year the Pistons traded me and John Tresvant to Cincinnati for Jim Fox and Happy Hairston. I was a little surprised when it happened, but I had known that something was up for a long time. When the season had begun I was playing with the starting unit, but as the year progressed my minutes dwindled. In fact, I remember one game where I didn't play until the last minute of the game when the contest was already decided. This went on for awhile, then Donnis put me back in the starting lineup and I played a lot of minutes. I could not put my finger on exactly what was going on, but I thought I might get traded.

"Donnis told me about it in his hotel room while we were on a road trip to Philadelphia. He simply explained that I had been traded to Cincinnati and that they expected me to be on their floor for their next game.

"I got weak in my knees. I had halfway expected the news, yet I wasn't quite sure what to think about it. A range of thoughts went through my mind. On one hand, I thought that maybe I had not played well enough for Detroit. But on the other, I knew that could not be true because Detroit had kept me on their team and I had been a starter for almost three years. I also figured that if Cincinnati wanted me then I must not be that bad. In the end I suppose the thing that bothered me was the fact that Detroit was saying they wanted somebody else more than they did me.

"After talking to Donnis, I went to my room, grabbed my bags, and caught the next flight to Cincinnati. It just so happened that George Allen was on the flight with me. He and I talked about the trade and George told me that being traded just might be the best thing. George had a wonderful way of building up a young man's confidence. He explained that trades are a part of professional sports and you can't take them personally. By the time I arrived in Cincinnati, I was determined to forget about Detroit and to make the best of this new situation."

"When I got to the stadium, Ed Jucker (the head coach) and I met. Ed explained the plays and assured me that he didn't expect that I would learn everything in one week. Later, I met my new teammates. They were friendly and went out of their way to make me feel comfortable. In the game that night, I didn't play. I sat on the bench watching and listening. But as I sat there, I began to get excited. I was on the same team as my childhood idol, Oscar Robertson, and I was almost afraid that this was a dream and at any moment I might wake up and find myself in a hotel in Philadelphia.

"As soon as I learned the plays, Ed put me in the starting five. I played in the backcourt with Oscar. The Royals needed more offense so I was able to make a contribution right away. Within a couple of weeks I felt quite comfortable with my teammates. I'd learned the plays and understood the fundamental strengths and weaknesses of the team. Away from basketball I was able to move my few belongings from Detroit to Cincinnati. I had no problem finding a place to stay. In fact, Jim Fox and I simply swapped apartments."

Tom made a major contribution to the Royals. With his help Cincinnati almost made the playoffs. Ironically, they lost the last playoff spot to Detroit on the last day of the season. In a doubleheader at the Cincinnati Gardens, Tom's former mates beat the Celtics, who were resting Bill Russell for the playoffs. Tom and the Royals lost to Dick and the Knicks, giving Detroit a trip to the playoffs against Boston, and sending Tom and his teammates home for the summer.

"You can never prove this kind of stuff, but I think Red (Auerbach) `tanked' that game with Detroit. I'm certain that he wanted to play Detroit instead of us in the playoffs," Tom speculates. "Cincinnati had beaten them in six of their last eight meetings and I think the last thing Red wanted to see was Oscar and the rest of us in a playoff."

* *

While Tom went through the experience of being traded, Dick and the Knicks played .500 basketball and made it to the playoffs. In 1967 the playoff format was as follows: the top four teams of each division went to the playoffs. (With the addition of Chicago, Seattle and San Diego both divisions had six teams.) The second and third place teams played each other in a seven game series to see who would earn the right to play the winner of the series between the first and fourth place team. The Knicks came in third behind Boston and Philadelphia. Thus, New York played Philly in a seven game series. The series went six games with Philadelphia prevailing.

"I had a horrible case of the flu so I barely played at all," Dick recalls. "With my health as poor as it was, I wasn't able to help my team. I don't remember much about the series except one incident that happened late in the last game. We were down by a couple of points and Red had called a timeout. He explained that he wanted Walt Bellamy to foul Wilt Chamberlain as soon as the ball came inbounds. (In those days there was no such thing as an intentional foul nor was it necessary to foul the person who had the ball.) Wilt was the Sixer's worst free throw shooter and Red wanted him on the line in the hope that he would miss. Wilt did not like it when teams did that to him and he wasn't a person you'd want to make mad. When the ball came into play, Bellamy, apparently worried about making Wilt mad by fouling him, did nothing.

"After the game, Red was all over Walt, wanting to know why he didn't foul Wilt. Bellamy just shrugged his shoulders and said: `I forgot.' I guess that's one of the things that made Wilt such a great player---he had a way of intimidating opponents into forgetting things."

* *

During the off-seasons Dick and Tom had started careers as stockbrokers. The twins spent their summers completing the courses required for certification and then went to work for E.F. Hutton (Tom) and Hayden and Stone (Dick).

"I knew that I would eventually have to find something to do with the rest of my life and I thought I might like to get into the brokerage business," Dick explains. "But once I got into it I decided that I'd better look for something else. Aside from the fact that I had to ride in on the subway wearing a suit and tie during the hot New York summer, I just didn't enjoy that type of interaction. I thought I wanted to work with people, but I wanted to do something other than selling securities."

"I felt the same way that Dick did," Tom agrees. "In fact, after I got settled in Cincinnati, I discovered that E.F. Hutton did not have an office in town and that ended my career as a stockbroker.

Chapter 7

The "Original Sun" (Photo courtesy Phoenix Suns)

In 1968 the NBA added two more teams: the Milwaukee Bucks and the Phoenix Suns. In adding Phoenix, the league took a calculated gamble. The Suns' franchise was located in area which had little experience with a professional sports franchise. Richard Bloch, Donald Pitt, and Don Diamond owned the club. They convinced Jerry Colangelo, a bright young general manager who had helped bring the Chicago Bulls into the league, to relocate in Phoenix and run their franchise.

Colangelo agreed and immediately set about finding a head coach. He chose Johnny "Red" Kerr who had enjoyed a long and successful tenure as a player. Kerr, in addition to having a wonderful sense of humor, possessed one of the brightest basketball minds of the day and represented an excellent choice for a key position.

With a general manager and a coach in place, the Phoenix franchise had but one more task to complete--- Colangelo and Kerr had to fill the roster. When the NBA added teams it held an expansion draft. Existing teams were permitted to "protect" eight players, while the other three were placed into the draft. In 1968, for example, the Bucks and the Suns were permitted to select eighteen players from this "expansion pool." They also received their normal allotment of college draft choices. From this pool of players plus any free agents they wanted to sign in pre-season tryouts, the Bucks and Suns formed their teams. Incidentally, the cost of a franchise in 1968 was two million dollars.

When Kerr and Colangelo sat down to talk about building the Suns, they quickly decided that they wanted to start with a few talented younger players to form a nucleus from which they could build a solid franchise.

"I knew we couldn't win the world championship in one season, but I thought we could be competitive right from the start," explains Colangelo who'd played college ball for Illinois. "When I looked at the expansion draft I hoped to find a few young players who had some experience and perhaps could play more than one position. I thought if I could get a couple of guys who fit that criteria, then maybe when Kareem (Lew Alcindor at the time) came out of college we would be in a position to draft him and already have the nucleus of the rest of the team intact.

"When I looked down the list of players available, I could not believe that Dick Van Arsdale's name was on that list. He and Fred Hetzel were the first two names that really jumped out at me. Fred had been a terrific scorer for Golden State (formerly San Francisco), but Dick represented all of those things we wanted in a player. He was a hard-nosed, no nonsense competitor. He could score and rebound and we could play him at guard or forward. We took him with our first pick."

The news that he'd been left unprotected and subsequently drafted by Phoenix shocked Dick. "I'd been starting for them almost from the day I arrived in town," Dick recalls. "So yes, I was shocked. When Eddie Donovan (Knicks' general manager) told me my initial reaction was disbelief. When I called Barb and I told her, she started crying. I could hardly blame her. The only thing we knew about Phoenix was that it was in a desert somewhere west of the Mississippi."

"I think the thing that threw me off was the fear of the unknown," Barb recalls. "I didn't know anything about Phoenix. I didn't know what this meant as far as Dick's playing career was concerned, or how long we'd be out there. One moment we were going to be in New York and then bang, we were moving to what I perceived to be the middle of nowhere."

"Dick was an important player for the Knicks and a good friend as well. I hated to see him go," recalls Bill Bradley who later helped lead the Knicks to a world championship. "I know he and Barb took the news hard, but I also knew that he would make the best of the situation. Dick was the type of player and person who was going to be successful no matter where he played."

"He was not in the best of spirits when I talked to him," adds Bill Shover, who had known the twins since he'd worked in public relations for the Indianapolis newspapers. Shover had moved to Phoenix in the early sixties to assume a similar position with the *Phoenix Republic* and *Gazette*. When the Suns came to town, Bill became a friend and adviser to Jerry Colangelo and he loudly applauded the GM's first choice. "Dick Van Arsdale was the perfect person with whom to start a franchise. I knew it, Jerry and Red knew it, but now we had to convince Dick Van Arsdale. When Dick and I talked on the phone he was still a little shocked. I tried to assure him that this was probably one of the best things that ever happened to him. I knew that if he and Barb gave Phoenix half a chance, they'd really enjoy it here.

"I'll never forget the day they flew out with their lawyer to meet with Jerry. It was in the middle of July and the valley was having one of the hottest summers on record. The temperature was at least 115 degrees. Dick and Barb weren't thirty minutes off the plane before each turned red as a beet. They both are fair-skinned and neither of them handled the heat very well."

"I won't forget that day either," Barb laughs. "I've never handled the heat well and when we got off that plane it felt like we'd stepped into an oven. I thought I'd never be able to live in such weather."

Despite their initial misgivings about moving to the

desert, Dick and Barb soon discovered that they could adjust to the climate and, within a short time, realized that they preferred Phoenix to New York.

"We rented a spacious condo with a pool," Barb recalls. "Our new home was twice as big as our apartment in New York had been and much more beautiful. It didn't take me long to find a teaching position and as the season changed from summer to fall the weather wasn't bad at all."

"I've always liked wide open spaces and we had plenty of that to look forward to," adds Dick. "I think our initial reaction to the move came as the result of not knowing anything about Phoenix. The scenery in the valley is beautiful and we both agreed that it was going to be easier to raise a family in Phoenix than it would be in New York. Aside from that, the people in the Suns' organization were nice and the situation was everything we could hope for and then some.

"Even so, while I quickly adjusted to the new environment, it took me awhile to get over what the Knicks had done to me. I came into their organization without a guaranteed contract. I stepped right into their starting lineup and made first team all rookie in my first season. During the next two seasons I continued to start and didn't complain when they signed other players to larger contracts. I worked hard to be a team member in that organization and I thought it was extremely disloyal of them to tell me one thing and then do something else. It would have been one thing for them to trade me somewhere, but to just let me go, that was something else. And while I did get over it I still believe that loyalty is something that should go both ways."

Dick describes his beginning with the Suns' organization as relationship built on mutual respect.

"After the expansion draft Jerry Colangelo and Richard Bloch (one of the owners) flew to New York and had lunch with me. They assured me that I figured big in their plans for the franchise and explained a little of what they were trying to do. Jerry was about twenty-eight at the time. He made a positive impression on me. Jerry had been involved with the Bulls' franchise and had a definite vision as to what was going to happen in Phoenix. He knew the professional game as well as any GM in the league and you could tell that he always did his homework. By the time our first season started, I had gotten to know him a little better and he's been one of my best friends ever since."

* *

Johnny Kerr, Jerry Colangelo, Dick Van Arsdale and the rest of the Phoenix Suns all realized that "Rome was not built in a day," nor would the Phoenix Suns become a dominating basketball team in one season.

"I guess you could say we hoped for the best and prepared for the worst," Dick recalls. "We didn't expect to make the playoffs and we knew we probably would lose more than we won. Red (Kerr) ruled us with a loose rein. He emphasized the same things all head coaches emphasize, but he also realized that we simply did not have the horses. He tried to make it fun. Red has a great sense of humor. He'd won coach of the year with the Bulls in his second season as a coach and he had a lot of self-confidence. He realized that we were in for a long season so he just tried to keep us as loose as he could."

The Suns' inaugural season got off to a great start, then sputtered, finally coming to a complete collapse. The team jumped out of the gate to a 3-1 record, slipped to 5-6 and then lost sixteen in a row. Their final record was 16-66, earning them a last place finish in the Midwest

Division.

While the team struggled, Dick emerged as one of the league's best players. On the strength of his twenty-one point scoring average and his tenacious defensive play (which led Sun fans to dub him "the flying Dutchman"), Dick was named to the Western Conference All-Star squad. "I was thrilled, absolutely thrilled. For me that was a pinnacle in my career. During my first three years in the league I felt I could play professional basketball, but in order to be among the best players I felt I had to raise the level of my game. In the off-seasons I had worked hard at honing my skills. Making the All-Star team was a great reward for all of that hard work.

"The Suns had suffered through a tough year and my making the All-Star team gave my teammates and the fans something to cheer about. I wasn't with the team for long before I realized coming to Phoenix was the best thing that had happened in my playing career. Red and Jerry believed in me and I was determined not to let them down. I think their attitude and the unselfish play of my teammates had a lot to do with my becoming an all-star.

"Jerry and the owners were quite proud that I'd been selected to the squad. Before I left town for the game they gave me three-hundred-dollars in spending money. By today's standards that seems like a paltry sum, but I thought it was a nice gesture.

"Tom did not make the team that year, but Jon McGlocklin did. He was playing in Milwaukee by then and he and I roomed together. We had a great time. I don't remember much about the game. I played about ten minutes, and the time went by so quickly, but the thrill of just being a part of that event stayed with me for the rest of the season."

* *

By virtue of their last place finish in the Midwest, the Suns earned a chance at the first pick in the 1969 college draft. The prize for the team holding the first pick would be an opportunity to sign Lew Alcindor. Alcindor had led UCLA to several national championships and most observers agreed that he would become the next dominating big man in professional basketball. The Suns and Milwaukee, the other expansion team, had both finished last, necessitating a coin toss to see which of the two teams would have the first pick. The Bucks won the toss, selected Alcindor and two years later won a world championship.

"The franchise has not had a lot of luck with coin tosses," Colangelo admits. "We lost the toss that would have given us Jabbar and, later, we lost another coin toss that would have brought us David Robinson. We got Neal Walk instead of Kareem. Neal was a fine player and gave us some excellent performances, but even Neal would have to admit that Kareem was a better pick."

In addition to Neal Walk, the Suns managed to add two other good players. They got Paul Silas from Atlanta for Gary Gregor and signed Connie Hawkins who had recently won a court case against the NBA. The league had banned him for allegedly not reporting a bribe offer he'd received while playing college ball at Iowa. Hawkins sued the league to lift the ban. He won and was quickly signed by the Suns.

"When we added Hawk, Silas, and Jimmy Fox we got better in a hurry," Dick explains. "Silas was great rebounder, Foxy could shoot, and Hawk could do things with a basketball that the rest of us didn't think was possible. I knew we were going to be more competitive," Dick recalls. "Red moved me out to guard with Gail Goodrich and we had Silas and Connie at forward. Foxy shared the center spot with our rookie, Neal Walk. We also picked up Jerry Chambers who had played on several of the Laker's good teams and Arty Harris.

"Colangelo did a heck of a job of making us competitive in a hurry. You can only wonder what would have happened if we had won that coin toss and picked Kareem."

All of the changes in personnel eventually led to a coaching change as well. Thirty-eight games into their second season the team was 15-23. The team had improved, but Jerry thought they needed a different direction. He released Kerr and took over as interim coach. The Suns responded. They played four games over .500 during the rest of season (24-20) and with a victory in San Diego in their next-to-the-last game clinched a spot in the playoffs.

"That was certainly a tumultuous season," Paul Silas recalls. "When I came over from Atlanta, I was quite excited because it looked as though I could step right into the starting five at Phoenix. I did start, but by mid-season the team was in turmoil, which led to a coaching change. After Jerry took over, we seemed to find better chemistry. Prior to his becoming coach, I think some of our problems had to do with a few of the changes that had taken place.

"Connie and I had stepped right in and taken roles that had belonged to other players during the previous season and I think the players and fans had liked Gary Gregor for whom I had been traded. It took awhile for all of us to get on the same page, but when we did we played some great basketball."

Having secured a playoff position, the Suns faced the mighty Los Angeles Lakers in their first playoff appearance. They were given little, if any, chance of winning. In fact, the LA papers referred to the team as "ten rejects and Connie Hawkins."

"I guess you could say we had not earned their respect yet," offers Dick. "After all the names Laker, Baylor, West, and Chamberlain had been around a lot longer than Silas, Goodrich, Hawkins, and Van Arsdale."

As predicted the Lakers easily handled the Suns in the first game 128-112. The Laker Triumvirate of Chamberlain, West, and Baylor did the bulk of the damage, scoring eighty-eight of their team's points, while Hawkins, Silas, and Van Arsdale combined for seventy. In the second game, the Suns shocked the Lakers and their Hollywood fans with a solid 114-101 victory. Hawkins scored thirty-four points and grabbed twenty rebounds while holding Wilt to "only" nineteen points.

Back home in Phoenix, the Suns punished the Lakers in a 112- 98 victory that saw Jim Fox, Connie Hawkins, and Paul Silas completely dominate inside. They held Chamberlain to eleven points and twelve rebounds, while the rest of the team overcame thirty-one and twenty point efforts from Jerry West and Elgin Baylor.

The fourth game, played in noisy Veteran's Memorial Stadium in front of a sellout crowd, saw the Suns jump out to a 19-2 advantage. They took that lead into the second quarter and never looked back. Their ten point (112-102) victory jolted Los Angeles like an earthquake. Suddenly the "rejects" from the valley of the sun had the Lakers down three games to one.

"As I look back at that series, it occurs to me that Phoenix did have quite a team," recalls Jerry West. "When the franchise came into being through the expansion draft, the talent in the league was not nearly as depleted as it has been for later expansion drafts. In 1968 there were quite a few quality players left unprotected so Phoenix had an opportunity to be competitive right from the start. Dick Van Arsdale and Gail Goodrich were two examples of the depth of talent in that draft. In addition to Dick and Gail, Connie Hawkins and Paul Silas were also two very good players. The Suns had gotten better in a hurry. Even so, at the start of that series, we didn't take them seriously.

"But by the time they had us down three games to one, they'd gotten our attention. We knew we were going to have to play better basketball or our season was going to be over."

Phoenix needed but one more victory to earn the right to play in the Western Conference final. And, as the series moved back to Los Angeles, the Suns even had history on their side---no team had ever come back from a 3-1 deficit.

As fate would have it, two things happened that turned the series around. "Jimmy Fox hurt his ankle and somewhere along the way somebody got Wilt mad," Dick recalls. "Foxy had done a great job on Chamberlain. When he injured his ankle we had to play Neal Walk, who was just a rookie. In game five Wilt really came to life. He scored thirty-six points, grabbed fourteen rebounds, blocked eight shots and was just about as intimidating as I've ever seen him." The Lakers manhandled the Suns 138-121, sending the series back to the valley for game six.

In the sixth game the Suns led 22-9 after the first eight minutes of play. But the Lakers, behind brilliant efforts from Keith Erickson and Dick Garrett, trimmed that lead to 26-22 by the quarter's end. From that point forward, West and Wilt took over. West scored thirty-five points and registered twelve steals, while Wilt grabbed twenty-six rebounds and dished out eleven assists.

Despite the Laker duo's powerful performances, the Suns held on until the bitter end. Going into the fourth quarter the contest was tied at 73-73 and the Lakers were unable to pull away until late in the final stanza when they put together a 9-0 run to lead 101-90. The Suns could not close the gap and fell 104-93.

"Mentally, I think some of us were gearing this one as a seventh game," Coach Colangelo explained in the post-game press conference. "I think that attitude caused a few of our guys to have the jitters---especially in the late stages of the fourth quarter." Colangelo then added that if the Lakers could win one in the midst of all the commotion caused by the 12493 Suns fans, then the Suns would have to follow that example and win one at the Forum under similar conditions.

Jerry's optimism, admirable as it was, could not change the grim reality of what was about to happen. The Suns had awakened a sleeping giant and now they were about to pay. In front of 17159 fans at the fabulous Forum, the Lakers scored the game's first eight points and continued to pour it on as they routed the second-year franchise 129-94. The chief culprit in ending the Suns' Cinderella story was Wilt Chamberlain. Chamberlain, apparently embarrassed or angered by the reviews of his performances in the LA and Phoenix papers, played the middle like a monster. He grabbed twenty-seven rebounds, blocked a dozen shots, and scored thirty points. Throughout the final game, "The Big Dipper" contested many of the Suns' shots, forcing them to alter their inside offense. In fact, Phoenix hit for only 32.4 percent from the field.

"When Wilt wanted to play hard, he was something else," Dick admits. "Earlier in the series he did not contest us nearly as much when we drove the lane. I guess we got him mad.

"Losing that series after we were up three games to one was heartbreaking. But for a second-year franchise to go toe-to-toe with the Lakers like we did was quite an accomplishment. We had nothing to be ashamed of."

Dick defends against Elgin Baylor in the 1970 playoffs.
(Photo courtesy Phoenix Gazette)

Chapter 8

Dick drives on Tom at the 1971 All-Star game
(Photo courtesy Phoenix Gazette)

While the Sun's playoff appearance surprised and pleased Dick and the fans in Phoenix, in Tom's corner of the world the Cincinnati Royals continued to flounder. In an effort to change the team's fortunes, management made a few changes. Prior to the start of the 1969-70 season, Bob Cousy, the Boston Celtic's legendary guard, who had moved out of professional basketball and into coaching at Boston College, replaced Ed Jucker as the Royals head coach. Shortly thereafter standout forward Jerry Lucas was traded to San Francisco for Jim King and Bill Turner.

"We had a pretty good team," Tom explains. "But we didn't have a dominating big man. The big center was a lot more important back then and when you didn't have one you had to constantly look for the right `chemistry.' I suppose that was one of the reasons for trading Jerry. He was an excellent team player and could do everything on the court, but I think he had a personality conflict with Cousy. The other factor might have been Lucas' business interests. He'd been talking like he might retire at the end of the season."

Without Lucas, even more of the scoring responsibilities fell on Tom's broad shoulders. He handled those responsibilities well. Despite his team's poor showing, Tom averaged nearly twenty-three points per game. One of the highlights of his second year in Cincinnati was a game against Los Angeles where he scored forty-one points. On the strength of such an outstanding season, Tom was named to the Eastern Conference All-Star team. He would play against his brother who made the Western squad for the second year in a row.

"I'll never forget getting the news that I'd made the all-star team," Tom recalls. "I couldn't help but think back to the conversation I'd had with George Allen on the flight to Cincinnati after I'd been traded. He was right. That trade resurrected my career. Ed Jucker and Bob Cousy believed in my abilities and gave me the opportunity to be a major contributor. I was grateful to them and planned to work as hard as I could to continue to be a factor on the team.

"Unfortunately, while I was enjoying my best year, my team was struggling. We only won two of our first eleven games. We did improve after that, but every time it looked as though we'd turned things around we'd lose a couple in a row and were right back where we started. This was especially difficult on Cousy. He'd played on all of those great Celtic teams and I think he thought he would be able to come right in and turn things around.

"The situation got so bad that Cousy, who was forty-one at the time, suited up and played seven games. He could still thread the needle with his passes, but he'd lost a lot of quickness and was ineffective on defense. We ended the season in fifth place (in a seven team division) twenty-four games behind New York. When the season was over I think we all knew that some changes were in order, but we were a little surprised at what those changes turned out to be."

In the summer of 1970, the Cincinnati Royals traded Oscar Robertson to the Milwaukee Bucks for Flynn Robinson and Charles Paulk. The move teamed the incomparable guard with the game's most-dominating-player-to-be, Lew Alcindor. The trade gave Oscar an opportunity to win a world championship and, for all intents and purposes, spelled the end of the Royals' franchise in Cincinnati.

At the time, however, Tom, one of the few veterans left in the Royals roster, tried to put the move in the best possible light. "I think it was good for him and for us," he told Barry McDermott of the Cincinnati Enquirer. "Why keep a guy when every reason you have him for doesn't do any good? Oscar was supposed to draw a lot of people to the Gardens, yet attendance is terrible every year. He was supposed to lead the Royals to a championship, but one guy can't do that.

"Oscar has but one goal left as a professional basketball player and that is to win a world championship. He's getting older and I don't think he believed that he could win one here. There was a time a few years ago when the Royals got off to a great start and were leading the league. During that time you could see the enthusiasm in his face. But as the team faltered and began to lose you could see the enthusiasm drain away.

"He's at a point in his career where he has to see a opportunity to win it all. He has that in Milwaukee and in exchange we got a couple of capable young players."

In looking back at the comments he made to the press on the heels of that trade, Tom stands by his assertion that the deal was in Oscar's best interest. But he sees the situation from Cincinnati's point of view in a different light. "The franchise was going nowhere," he explains. "Oscar wanted that world championship and he was becoming more and more disenchanted with the situation. He and Cousy did not seem to get along very well and, when the team continued to lose, their rift became deeper. If anything, the Royals' hand was forced. Oscar wanted out and his contract permitted him to choose to go to wherever he wanted. He chose Milwaukee, and the Royals were left to make the best of whatever they could get in exchange for him."

With Oscar gone, Tom became the captain of 1970-71 Cincinnati Royals. He led by example with a 22.9 scoring average. The team, however, finished third in a four team division. (In 1970 the league added Buffalo and Portland and divided the East and West into four divisions. The Atlantic: New York, Philadelphia, Boston, and Buffalo; the Central: Baltimore, Atlanta, Cincinnati, and Cleveland; the Midwest: Milwaukee, Chicago, Phoenix, and Detroit; and the Pacific: Los Angeles, San Francisco, Seattle, San Diego, and Portland.)

Ironically, during the same season Dick was named the Suns captain. He led his team in scoring with a 21.9 average, and both he and Tom made the all star team.

One of the keys to Tom's increasing stature as a professional player was the guidance of Bob Cousy. "There's no doubt that Bob had a tremendous effect on me as a player," says Tom. "Cousy would often pull me aside and complain about the way I held the ball, when I shot it or how I could have made a good play even better. He was a perfectionist and he didn't hesitate to let you know if he thought you ought to be doing something better. The night I scored forty-one points he was on me after the game because of a shot I passed up and a open man I missed. He was always trying to get us to do things better. Perhaps the greatest contribution he made to my game was to teach me how to use a head fake to get myself a better shot.

"When I came into the league, if my defender was not in my face and I was within seventeen feet of the basket, I'd set up and shoot. That drove Cousy crazy. He wanted me to use a fake to get the defensive man to commit, giving me an opportunity to either take the shot or drive around him for a better shot. When I started doing that I increased my shooting percentage and scored more points."

In addition to Cousy's helpful pointers on how to play the game, he helped Tom's confidence by building the team's offense around him. "If you had five Tom Van Arsdales you'd be in pretty good shape in this league," Cousy once told the press in a post-game interview. "One of the great things about Tommy is that he is a team player. I don't have to worry about him putting the ball up too much or under the wrong circumstances. He's a positive influence out on the floor, especially for our younger players. We try to get the ball into his hands as much as possible."

"Tommy was a great basketball player and a great person. He and Dick are prototypes of the all-american boy," Cousy insists, adding that Tom was one of a few bright spots in his professional coaching career. "I had coached college basketball for several years and when I came to the pros the one thing I missed the most was the hustle of those college kids. As a professional coach I could not understand why some of my players---guys who were making twice what I made when I was playing--- could not give one-hundred percent every night. But Tommy Van Arsdale was not that way. He was an over-achiever. I think he got the most out of his God-given talent every time he stepped out on the floor.

"He was our team leader, but he didn't do it with a lot of words and speeches. He did it by diving after balls and skinning his knees. When the troops see the captain scrapping for every loose ball, they respond. He embarrassed his teammates into playing harder.

"I never got to know Tommy much socially, but he always impressed me as someone who carried the same qualities that made him a good basketball player into his life away from the court. I've been around great athletes all of my life and I know they are usually pampered along the way. Many carry an attitude that they don't have to behave like normal people. This was not the case with Tommy and Dick. They were gentlemen. Their parents must have been mighty proud of them."

* *

After the third place finish in '70-71, the Royals opened their 1971-72 campaign amid rumors and speculation that the team would be moved. Attendance over the past six or seven years had steadily declined and the team was reportedly losing too much money. While the front office pondered the team's future, the Royals got off to a good start---especially Tom. After nine games the Royal's captain carried a hefty twenty-eight point scoring average, placing him third behind Kareem and Bob Love in the league scoring race. However, in another one of those cruel twists of fate, Tom suffered an injury that would not only cause him to miss several games, but would leave him scarred for life.

In a game against Golden State, Tom got caught between the Warrior's Fritz Williams, who had gone airborne on a layup attempt, and Nate Williams, who also had jumped to block the shot. The two collided with Tom in the middle, sending Tom to the floor where Nate Williams landed on top of him.

"After I landed, Nate landed on me and suddenly I felt a numbness in my arms," Tom recalls. "I couldn't move my hands and everything felt like pins and needles."

The cause of Tom's numbness was traced to bruises on the seventh and eighth vertebrae, which are located in the upper portion of the spine. The bruised spine led to a temporary paralysis of Tom's arms and also brought on a great deal of pain. "I think it was the first time I'd ever been given a sedative. I'd been hurt before, but never as bad. Once, in a game in Boston, I swung out my left arm on my way up for a layup and I felt a sharp pain in my forearm. I'd smacked George Patterson, a teammate, right in the mouth and one of his front teeth was imbedded in my arm. I remember that incident well because the Celtics' team doctor sewed me up without even sterilizing the wound. By the time we were on the airplane headed for home my arm had swelled to the size of a softball.

"I'd also had some problems with my knees, but, as I said, the paralysis business was scary. In the past several months several sport-related injuries had occurred, one resulting in a death. (Chuck Hughes from the Detroit Lions professional football team had died during a game in Detroit and Ken Dyer from Cincinnati had been paralyzed in a football related accident.) It got me to thinking about things other than basketball.

"When I finally did get the feeling back in my arms it took a week or so for me to regain my strength. In just the short time that I'd been in the hospital, the muscles in my arm had atrophied. After I went back to playing, my shot was off which caused me to lose a little confidence. However, I did finally manage to adjust. I made the all star team again and I think I ended up scoring about twenty points per game (19.2). In fact, late in the season I had a forty-four point effort against San Diego. By the end of the year, I felt as though I'd completely overcome the problem, but even today I continue to have a little numbness in my arms."

While Tom struggled to overcome his spinal injury, the Royals continued to struggle both in the standings and at the gate. Late in the season the team announced that it would indeed be leaving Cincinnati. In 1972-73 the Royals would be playing in Kansas City and Omaha. Cincinnati residents greeted the news of the team's departure with the same attitude they'd displayed to its presence. A nucleus of hard-core fans were devastated, but the majority of the city did not care.

"I think Cincinnati is a provincial city," offers Connie Dierking, who played college basketball for the University of Cincinnati and later starred at center for the Royals for five seasons. "People from Cincy wanted the team to be owned by locals. Unfortunately, the team was owned by the Jacobs family from Buffalo, New York. They'd moved the team from Rochester back in the late 1950s.

"I don't think fans were as loyal to the team as they would have been if it had been owned by people from Cincinnati and the Jacobs' family never went out their way to endear themselves to the city. In addition to that, when Cousy came in as coach he got rid of every veteran except for Tom Van Arsdale. After he arrived, the franchise was a revolving door for players. Every year the fans had to reacquaint themselves with a new version of the Royals, which wasn't conducive to creating loyal followers.

"When they let Oscar go, that was the last straw. Axelson (the GM) made a lousy deal and then tried to convince fans that it was in the team's best interest. Royals' fans were many things, but they weren't stupid. That deal was the end of the line. I think Cincinnati could support a franchise, but not the one that left town in 1972. Fans here were glad to see them go."

The players, on the other hand, were livid about the plan to play home contests in two different cities. Chief among the critics of this proposal was team captain Tom Van Arsdale. "I wasn't opposed to the move so much as I was opposed to the way things were going to be done," he explains. "Joe Axelson had told us that Kansas City would be the home of the new franchise, but then added that we would only be playing twenty-one games at Kansas City's Municipal Stadium. The rest of our home games would be played in Omaha.

"I just thought it was a `bush league' to move the franchise and then send us on the road for sixty-one games. It made the NBA look like a minor league again. Playing home games in two different cities was something I thought the league had moved beyond. How can you consider a franchise to be major league when it can't even schedule a full compliment of home games in its home city?"

Tom's outspoken criticism was seconded by many of his teammates, but did not endear him to fans in his new "hometown" nor in Omaha. "I've no regrets about any of the things I said," says Tom who moved from Cincinnati to Phoenix at the end of the '71-72 season. "I didn't mind playing in Kansas City nor in Omaha. Any one of the two would have been fine for me. I just thought management was doing a poor job of helping the team. In fact, I was becoming more and more disenchanted with the way things in the franchise were going. When I left at the end of the season, I hoped things would get better, but I had a feeling that my days as a Royal were numbered."

When the Royals opened their 1972-73 season, Tom was in the starting lineup, but his playing time was considerable less than what it had been during the previous season. "I think Cousy wanted to take the team in a different direction," Tom surmises. "Nate Archibald became the more influential player on the floor. Nate was a great player, but I think they gave him too much of a free rein."

"As the season progressed, I saw my minutes going down and down so I went to Cousy and asked to be traded. This was my eighth year in the league and I thought I still could be a major contributor somewhere. I wasn't happy with the Royals. They were having one of those youth movements where they wanted to give the younger players more time and I was in the prime of my career. It was obvious that I was not in their future plans.

"Cousy said he'd do what he could. I knew that eventually they would get rid of me. I had moved to Phoenix during the off-season and was hoping to get traded to them. When Bob told me that I'd been traded to Philadelphia I was shocked. They were having one of the worst seasons in the history of the NBA. When the trade was announced they had a 4-47 record. Roy Rubin had started the season as coach, but by the time I arrived Kevin Loughery had taken over. To say the least, it was not one of the happiest days in my career, but I tried to put the situation in the proper perspective. I left Kansas City determined to go to Philadelphia and do all I could to help turn the franchise around."

"What bothered me most about Tom's career was that whenever Tom got traded he was traded to a team with a worse record than the one he left," says Dick. "I've always thought that he deserved a better fate. The deal with Philadelphia was absolutely the worst. But Tom didn't complain. He always maintained a positive attitude. He went to Philadelphia and played to the best of his abilities."

Kevin Loughery had only been in Philly for four days when he made the deal that brought Tom to the Sixers. "I respect John Block (they traded him and a future draft choice for Tom), but we need a quick forward and we got one in Van Arsdale," Loughery explained to *Philadelphia Enquirer* reporter John Dell. "We plan to stress defense and Tom plays great defense and puts points on the board, too. He'll fit in quite nicely with what we want to do."

Tom was in the starting lineup for the Sixers next game. He scored twenty-four points, but the Sixers lost 101-96 to Buffalo. "There isn't a team in the league that wouldn't want him and most of them probably made offers for him," offered Buffalo coach Jack Ramsey, commenting on Philadelphia's newest acquisition. But even with Tom Van Arsdale the Sixers continued to flounder. Along the way they dropped a record twenty-one games in a row. They finally ended their skid by beating the New York Knickerbockers in front of a small, loyal hometown crowd.

"The way they applauded us you'd of thought we'd won the world championship," Tom laughs. "People talk about Philadelphia crowds as being tough on players, but that year they were mostly sympathetic. And you would have expected the team to be divisive and in disarray, but that wasn't true either. We all got along. My locker was next to Fred Carter, who started at guard and he was always telling me that the team needed to stay positive. Fred Boyd, John Trapp, Leroy Ellis, Dale Schleuter, and the rest of the team, was as close a group of guys as any team I had played on.

"They told me that Rubin, the former coach, had put them through the weakest training camp they'd ever had. They started the season out of shape and things just got worse from there. Loughery came in with the opposite attitude. He had us running the floor for the entire game. So that, too, was an adjustment. By the end of the season we were 9-73 and owned the distinction of having the worst record in the history of the NBA.

"I'll never forget the final game of the year. We were playing Detroit in Pittsburgh. I packed all of my things in the car and drove to the game so I could head out for Phoenix as soon as it was over. The locker room wasn't particularly jolly that night. The team was eager to finish the season. We certainly hadn't planned any post-game celebrations. Anyway, before Loughery came down to talk to us, the trainer, Al Domenico stood up and said: `Don't anybody get hurt tonight and for godsake don't call any timeouts. Let's get this over with as quickly as possible.' That got us all laughing. I don't know if it was a fitting ending or not, but we lost again that night to the Pistons. The drive home to Phoenix after that game was one of the longest rides in my life. But was I ever glad to have that season behind me."

Tom drives against Detroit's Curtis Rowe.
(Photo courtesy Ed Baxter)

Chapter 9

Jill, Jason, Barb, and Dick - Christmas 1991

While it seemed that Tom was destined to travel from team to team, Dick became the captain and cornerstone of the Suns' franchise. The fans and management admired his tenacious style of play, and he and Barbara discovered that they enjoyed living in the valley of the sun. Within a year of arriving, Dick found himself immersed in the social and business life of the valley as well.

Among his first new friends and business associates in Phoenix were Jon and Jimmy Walker. "I met Jimmy during the early part of our first season. He was the president of the Suns fan club. I first met him at one of their functions. Jimmy introduced me to his brother Jon and somewhere along in there they both met Tom. One of my most special memories of Jon is summed up in a picture we took of the three of us with our very first fishing boat. We had all chipped in and bought this small bass boat. With all three of us in it, I think we could have just about sunk the thing, but at the time it was among our most prized possessions."

"When we first heard that Phoenix was going to get a professional basketball franchise, we were excited," recalls Jimmy Walker, who has been in the insurance and securities business in Phoenix for over twenty years. "In 1968 Arizona was still considered to be in the middle of nowhere, therefore, we figured a pro ball club would bring the city a little national exposure. And we were just delighted in knowing that all those other professional basketball teams were going to be playing in our town.

"When the team selected Dick as its first player, I didn't know much about him except that he was half of the famous Van Arsdale twins from Indiana and that he'd been hesitant to come out here. When we first met, I couldn't help but be impressed with the guy. Sports personalities are often aloof and distant, but not Dick. He was as down home friendly as any person I've ever met.

"And on the basketball court he was something else to see," adds Jim's brother Jon. "During those early seasons, the team was poor and not many fans showed up at the games. Even so, Dick would fight for loose balls and play every minute as though the game was for a world championship. The fans loved him.

"I believe that aside from Jerry Colangelo, Dick Van Arsdale was the most important reason for the franchise being as successful as it is today. He set a standard for basketball players in this town that is second to none."

While Dick was enjoying his best years as a player he realized that his days playing basketball were numbered and continued to look for career opportunities away from the game. After his second year in Phoenix, he took a part-time job with a local television station co-anchoring a morning show called Arizona Today. He also did a sports segment for the five o'clock news.

"I was looking for things that I might want to do when I retired and I thought I might like to get into television," Dick explains. "But I wasn't at the job for long before I decided that I didn't like it enough to pursue it as a career. Even so, I learned a lot about television. I had to write my own sports stories and preparing for those live interviews on the morning show was a challenge.

"Even though I decided against making television my second career, the experience wasn't all that bad and it helped prepare me for my years as a color commentator. While I worked at KTAR, I met some nice people and the work environment was fun. My co-workers were a lively bunch. I remember one incident where my co-host for the Arizona Today, Diane Kalas, put me up to doing a interview with a lady who was supposed to have collected unique rocks from lake Michigan. I was on the set making an earnest effort to find out what it was about these pieces of gravel that was so interesting while Diane and the staff were backstage laughing their heads off. She'd set me up with a fake interview.

"Another time one of my co-workers was drunk and during my sports segment he crawled up in front of me out of camera range and put his hand up on my desk. I started laughing while we were on the air. Those studios are not at all like what people watching the TV think they are like. Sometimes the atmosphere resembles a zoo, which makes it awfully difficult to concentrate on what you are doing.

"I tried working in television for awhile, but then I turned to real estate, which I found much more to my liking."

* *

The year 1970 brought many changes for Dick and Barbara. They were blessed with a beautiful baby daughter Jill. Unfortunately, months before Barbara gave birth her mother suddenly died.

"1970 was quite a year for me," Barb recalls. "My mother, who was as dear a person I have ever known, died when I was still pregnant with Jill. She died from an aneurism and it happened quite suddenly. I was devastated. I was her only child and she and I were extremely close. I was still mourning her loss when Jill was born.

"With a baby in the house I was busier than I'd ever been before. While my thoughts were still with my mother, I was beginning to learn to deal with her absence through the everyday process of tending to Jill.

"Dick was a great support during this trying time in my life. A professional basketball player leads a hectic life during the season, but Dick was with me as much as he could be and he helped with Jill, especially during the times when the team was at home and he had his days free. He wasn't great about getting up at night, but he did change his fair share of diapers and spent quite a few afternoons babysitting rather than on the golf course."

"Irene's death had a profound effect on our household," Dick acknowledges. "She and Barb had a great relationship. Irene had been a positive influence in my life, too. Barb and I were looking forward to making her a proud grandparent so the suddenness of her passing stunned us.

"I was concerned about Barb because her's had not been an easy pregnancy and now she had this other burden to bear. I was concerned, but I was also proud of her. She responded to the situation by maintaining a positive attitude.

"I'll never forget the day Jill was born. The nurses had placed a makeshift basketball goal over Jill's crib. Jill, just a tiny baby, lay there. She was crying at the top of her voice. I've always said that she had the healthiest lungs of any baby I've heard.

"Becoming a parent was one of those things that I had expected would happen sometime in my life, but when it did I began to realize what a wonderfully special thing it is. Anyway, as I stood in that hospital room watching my daughter in her crib, I was as happy as I've ever been.

"The adjustment to having a new child in our home came with only a few problems. Barb understood that my work required me to travel and she didn't complain or try to make me feel guilty about not being around as much as I wanted to be. I've always thought the world of my wife, but I was especially proud of the way she handled becoming a mother. Barb has always been independent and I knew I didn't have to worry about her and the children. Although when she was pregnant with Jill, I did tell her that I didn't want a boy because I was afraid that I'd come home from road trips and find my son wearing dresses."

Three years later Dick and Barb had a son. His birth was more complicated than Jill's, but by the time he came home he, too, was a healthy child.

"When our second child, Jason, was born in 1973, Dick had to leave for a game in Houston. Unfortunately, not long after he left, Jason's lung punctured," Barb recalls. "This was a frightening development. They put him in an incubator and he had tubes in his mouth and IVs in his arms. Of course I was quite upset when I called Dick in Houston and told him what happened."

Dick remembers that phone call vividly. "I hadn't been off the plane for more than an hour when I got the call. I got right back on a plane and headed back for Phoenix. When Jason was first born I had thought he looked a little blue. I mentioned it to his nurses and apparently he suffered from something called Pnueamothorax. Unfortunately, they discovered the hole in the lung after I'd left."

"Seeing Jason with all of those tubes in his lungs and his tiny chest heaving for air gave us a tremendous fright, but everything turned out ok. He came home with us within a week and was a healthy boy."

Raising children found Dick and Barb in all of the typical dilemmas encountered by parents. "They both got into their fair share of trouble," Barb confesses. "I suppose the worst thing that happened occurred when Jill wandered out the back door and nearly drowned in the swimming pool. I'd put her in high chair to feed her and then went to answer the door and then the phone started ringing. While I was on the phone I had a premonition that something was not right. The kitchen was too quiet. When I looked, Jill was not in her high chair and the back door was open. I ran outside and sure enough she was in the pool floating on her back, gagging on the water as it lapped over her head. I dove in and grabbed her.

"She was still conscious, but had swallowed quite a bit of water. The incident nearly scared me to death, but Jill was all right. I didn't know if I should tell Dick about what had happened. After all everything had turned out all right and I didn't want to worry him while he was on the road. But, fearing he might hear about it secondhand, I called him. Since I was still somewhat shaken I was more dramatic than I needed to be.

"When I heard the tone of her voice, I feared the worst," Dick admits. "I was relieved to hear that Jill was just fine. Shortly after that I told Cotton Fitzsimmons, who was coaching the Suns at that time, what had happened. Ever since then Cotton calls Jill `Florence' in reference to the great English swimmer Florence Chadwick."

* *

On the basketball court, Dick and the Suns enjoyed a few winning seasons, but failed to make the playoffs. Dick made the all-star team in 1970 and 1971. During his first few seasons with the Suns, he had earned a reputation as someone who refused to back away from any challenge. "I used to call him `mad dog,'" quips Connie Hawkins who played for four seasons with Dick and the Suns. "Sometimes when Dick would drive down the lane, if he got fouled and the ref didn't call it---watch out. He'd get this look in his eye. His face would get all red and he would go back on defense hollering at the ref all the way. The next time he had the ball Dick would head for the basket and if you were in his way, then you were going to get run over. He was as a fierce competitor as I have ever played with.

"We had enforcers back in those days just as they have them today. These were guys who'd just as soon punch you as shake your hand. I learned to give such players a wide berth, but not Dick. He'd challenge them. If some 6'9" goon knocked him to the floor, Dick would get up and go after him."

"I used to tell my players not to make Wilt Chamberlain mad," recalls Cotton Fitzsimmons, who took over as coach of the Suns in 1970. "If you didn't make Wilt look bad on defense, then sometimes he wouldn't hurt you quite as bad on offense. This philosophy never sat well with Dick Van Arsdale. I think Dick resented the fact that he had to work so hard for everything and Wilt had so much height and talent that he hardly had to work at all. Dick would drive the lane against Wilt every chance he got, and Wilt would go after him. I think Dick Van Arsdale is one of the only guys whose shot Wilt always contested."

"I was in the Laker locker room before a game once, and the coach was giving the team their defensive assignments. When he got to Dick Van Arsdale's name he said, `Who wants to guard Van Arsdale?' His question was met with silence," recalls Bill Shover. "Nobody wanted to guard him. I'll never forget that because during the game somebody fell down in front of Dick while he was driving to the basket and Dick just stepped on the guy and continued down the lane."

* *

When Cotton Fitzsimmons came to Phoenix in 1970, it marked the beginning of one of the most successful coaching careers in the history of professional basketball. Cotton had coached under Tex Winter at Kansas State where he learned the triple-post offense, which Cotton then introduced to the pros.

"If you look at the evolution of offenses in the NBA, I think you have to count Cotton as one of the key innovators," Dick offers. "The triple-post was one of the first offenses that was a complete system. Before Cotton came along we generally had a few plays designed to isolate a player one-on-one, but the triple was more of a continuous motion where what the defense was doing would determine which play you ran. I liked the triple because it gave me number of options when I was bringing the ball upcourt."

"I'd learned the triple from Tex and was able to use it in Phoenix because it required an excellent passing center to work well. Neal Walk was that type of center," explains Cotton. "The key to the offense is spacing. Ideally, the three players on the strong side should form a triangle with about fifteen feet between each player. The center represented one point in the triangle, the guard/forward in the corner another, and the guard up top the third. The passing between these three would either permit one of them to find an open shot or act as a smoke screen for the two weakside players who looked for back door opportunities."

"With the triple-post we averaged more points per game and forced our opponents to play a more aggressive style of defense," adds Dick. "We also won more games. We were 48-34 in Cotton's first season and improved to 49-33 in his second, but both years we failed to make the playoffs."

"In 1971 we were in the Midwest division and placed third behind Milwaukee and Chicago. The Bucks had Kareem, McGlocklin, Oscar, Dandridge and Allen. They won well over sixty games. The Bulls, too, were loaded with talent. They had Bob Love, Jerry Sloan, Chet Walker, and Tom Boerwinkle. We had the fifth best record in the league and didn't make the playoffs. In 1972 the same thing happened. After that season I think Jerry decided we needed to change a few things. Among the changes were a new head coach and the emergence of Charlie Scott as our premiere player. Butch Von Breda Koff replaced Cotton and we also traded Paul Silas to Boston to get the rights to Charlie who was playing in the ABA."

"I loved Phoenix and at the time I hated to leave," admits Silas, who went on to win a couple of world championships with Boston. "I enjoyed playing for Cotton and with Dick and Connie and the rest of the Suns. Jerry did a great job out there and my wife and I hoped we'd be in Phoenix for a long time. But in the end the trade worked out to be one of the best things that ever happened for me."

While Colangelo has never been one to rest on his laurels, the changes in the 1972-73 Suns did not produce the results he expected. Jerry began to realize this almost before it happened. Von Breda Koff only coached seven games and then Colangelo took over.

"Butch had been a successful college coach at Princeton and he brought the same basic offense he used with those Ivy-leaguers to the pros," explains Dick. "It was a difficult offense to run because it was based on spontaneity. We were all supposed to be playing off of each others moves and so forth. This would have been great if we'd all been playing together for a long time, but such was not the case."

"Jerry came in after seven games and coached us the rest of the season. He was not what you would call an X's and O's type of coach. He was more of a players' coach.

Jerry tried to keep us loose and confident, but that season was a total loss. We went from winning forty-nine games to winning only thirty-eight."

John MacLeod stepped in as the Suns' next coach. A native Hoosier from Clarksville, Indiana, MacLeod had coached for six years at Oklahoma and brought with him yet another offensive scheme.

"John was another innovator," Dick recalls. "He brought in a passing game that used a lot of motion and keyed on looking for an open shot. His offense was more like what you see in the NBA today. The emphasis was on moving the ball around to find an open shot."

During the next two seasons the Suns did not improve. In fact, they got worse. The team's 30-52 record in '73-74 and 32- 50 mark in '74-75 would have seemed to indicate that another coaching change was imminent. But this time, Colangelo was patient. He was willing to give MacLeod more time to turn the team around. Jerry's patience paid off in a big way.

The 1975-76 Phoenix Suns will always be remembered as a group of over-achievers who defied the odds. The team had lost fifty games in '74-75 and many prognosticators, placing blame on MacLeod's emphasis on a passing offense and Colangelo's apparent ineptness at putting the team together, predicted a last place finish for the Suns.

During the off-season, however, Colangelo and MacLeod made several key personnel changes. Among the first of those changes came through the college draft. The team used its picks to get Alvan Adams and Rickey Sobers. Adams gave the Suns a talented center the caliber of Neal Walk who had been traded earlier to New Orleans for Dennis Awtrey and Curtis Perry. In Sobers, the Suns' added a quick guard with excellent defensive skills and mental toughness. In addition to the two draft picks, the Suns made a controversial deal that sent scoring ace Charlie Scott to Boston in exchange for Paul Westphal.

"I think it was the best deal we'd ever made," Dick offers. "The worst trade was the one that sent Paul Silas to Boston for Charlie and the best trade was the one that brought Paul Westphal here and sent Charlie back to Boston. I have nothing against Charlie Scott; he was a great ball player. But while he was in Phoenix he was a disruptive force on the team. Chemistry is vital in team sports and with Charlie on the team our chemistry was not very good."

After the start of the season, the team added Gar Heard and veteran guard Pat Riley. Even so, the Suns did not get out to a brilliant start. They quickly fell to last place in their division and languished there throughout the first months of the season. As they struggled, MacLeod and Colangelo faced increased criticism over the changes they had made.

"At the beginning of the season I don't think Jerry and I would have won any popularity contests," MacLeod admits. "But we weren't second-guessing ourselves. We thought we did what was best for the team and we hoped we could turn it around by the end of the year."

While the Suns were mired in last place with a 19-27 record at the All-Star break, the rest of the division was not doing much better. In fact, it began to appear as though a .500 record just might put a team in the playoffs.

Then, in late February the Suns' fortunes took another ominous turn. In a game against the New Orleans Jazz in the Superdome, Dick went up for a layup and had his legs cut out from under him by his defender, Ron

Behagen. Dick stuck out his arms to break the fall and in the process broke a bone in his left forearm.

"When Prosk (the Suns' venerable trainer Joe Proski) came out, he took one look at my arm and told me that I'd broken it. That was the most disappointing news I had heard in all my years as a player. I'd been in the league now for eleven years and the worst thing that had happened until then had been a torn calf muscle.

"We weren't out of the playoff picture at the time. In fact, by stringing together a few victories, we could still have been in great shape. I was on the downhill side of my career then, but I was still a big factor on our team and I hoped my absence wouldn't hurt us."

"Van's injury really put a fright in me," MacLeod recalls. "As a coach, a player like Van Arsdale spoils you. He does so many good things for the team, but you don't really notice it until you need him on the floor and he can't answer the call. Dick was the team captain and he made my job so much easier. If we needed a basket, he'd get the ball and drag his man down the lane for a layup. If the momentum had turned against us, he'd scrap for a steal or get on the floor and fight for a loose ball. These are things that don't always show up in box scores, but are essential to winning big games. I thought losing Van was the last thing we needed to have happen."

Odd as it might sound, Dick's absence did not hurt the team- --in a way it helped. "Ricky Sobers was a rookie that year and when Van went down Sobers took his spot in the lineup," explains Joe Gilmartin, a reporter for the Arizona Republic. "Rickey saw a lot of playing time from that point forward, which really helped when the team got to the playoffs. We lost Van for twenty-four games. Ricky filled in nicely and then we got Van back for the playoffs. It was almost as though we picked up another player along the way."

"I know it must have been difficult for Dick to sit on the bench with his arm in a cast when he wanted to be on the court," offers Sobers, who had played college ball at UNLV. "But he was my number one supporter. He'd talk to me when I did things wrong and explain how to play against certain players. Dick was always a team player and I appreciated the way he responded to being injured. He certainly helped me to be a much better player and he also showed a mental toughness that I greatly admired."

"Ricky was my type of player," says Dick. "He liked to play defense and he was as tough as nails. I enjoyed watching him because, even as a first year player, he showed the toughness of a veteran. The old pros didn't always appreciate his tenaciousness. They'd get in his face and expect him to back down, but he wouldn't. He was a fighter and I loved to see that in a young player."

The broken arm cost Dick twenty-four games, but he was with the team enough in the later stages of the season to get back in shape. By that time it looked as though the Suns might even make the playoffs. At the end of the year the team was 42-40. One of only three teams in the Western Conference to have better than a .500 record, they did indeed make the playoffs, facing the Seattle Supersonics, who had finished just one game better than the Suns at 43-39.

The Supersonics featured "downtown" Freddie Brown, seven-foot two-inch center Tom Burleson, and the diminutive Slick "Watts. The series started in Seattle where the Suns split the first two games, losing the first 102-99 and then winning the second 116- 111.

When the series moved to Phoenix for the next two games, the Veterans Memorial Coliseum was sold out for both contests, which Phoenix won 103-91 and 130-114.

Leading the series three games to one, the Suns headed back to Seattle where they lost 114-108. They then ended the series in front of their fans at the Coliseum with a decisive 123-112 victory.

The upset victory over Seattle placed them in the conference finals against the defending world champion Golden State Warriors. The Warriors, led by a resurgent Rick Barry who had returned after defecting to the ABA, were said to be basketball's next "dynasty" team. In addition to Barry, they featured Phil Smith, Clifford Ray, Jeff Mullins, and Keith Wilkes. Golden State had crushed the Washington Bullets four games to zero in the previous year's championship series and most observers believed that Phoenix could expect the same treatment.

The series opened in Oakland where the Warriors immediately served notice that they fully intended to defend their title against the East. They blasted the Suns 128-103 in a rout that saw the Suns commit thirty turnovers. In the second game, Rick Barry lit Phoenix up for forty-four points, but Paul Westphal and Alvan Adams countered his scoring with fine performances. Westphal scored thirty-one and Adams contributed nine assists as the Suns won 108-103, tieing the series at one game apiece.

The series moved to Phoenix for the next two games. In game three Golden State won back the home court advantage with a 99-91 victory. Now, trailing two games to one, the Suns were in desperate need of a victory. Behind a solid effort from Dick Van Arsdale, they got the win they needed. In game four, Dick had his best outing of the playoffs. He scored twenty points and helped his team to a 133-129 double overtime victory. "I was finally at a point where I felt like I was completely back from my injury. I realized that this might be my only chance at a world championship and I was a little more psyched up than usual. In the overtimes, I wanted the ball. I thought I could beat Phil to the basket, and when I did I either got a layup or found one of my teammates open on a switch. After being down for such a long time, I was happy to be contributing."

Game five was played back in Oakland where the Warriors again pounded Phoenix 111-105. As was generally the case, Rick Barry did the bulk of the damage, scoring thirty-eight points. Game six found the Suns back in Phoenix, facing elimination. With their backs against the wall, the team fought Golden State even for three quarters, then pulled ahead in the fourth. Leading by as many as eight, the Suns were forced to hang on for dear life when Keith Wilkes and Phil Smith went on a tear and cut the lead to two with less than a minute remaining. Clutch shooting from veterans Keith Erickson and Gar Heard saved the Suns, as they hung on for a thrilling 105-104 victory.

The seventh and final game was played in Oakland. The final contest between the two teams got off to a frenetic start and then exploded with a fight between Ricky Sobers and Rick Barry. The flare-up resulted in a bench-clearing brawl with players flying all over the press in the first row. The Suns' Curtis Perry sustained the most damage in the fracas as several fans literally pulled him over the press table and pummeled him in the back. When the referees finally restored order, both Sobers and Barry were penalized with technical fouls. The game resumed in a more orderly fashion until the second period when a fan tossed a golf ball at Sobers, who was roundly booed every time he touched the ball. Fortunately, the golf ball missed Ricky and bounced harmlessly across the court.

Aside from the fights and the rowdy fans, the game quickly turned into a contest of wills. The Suns struggled to run their pattern offense, while Golden State turned again and again to their scoring aces Charlie Johnson and Rick Barry. The two combined for twenty-four first-half points. The Warriors led by as many as eight points (26-18), but Phoenix fought back and even held a brief 37-36 advantage before Golden State pulled away to a six point lead at halftime (48-42).

Trailing by eight early in the third period, the Suns rallied behind excellent offensive and defensive rebounding. On defense, Rookie of the Year Alvan Adams blocked eleven Warrior shots and the guard play of Westphal, Van Arsdale, and Sobers stopped Golden State from using their "Go, Go" offense, which usually resulted in easy Warrior baskets. By the end of the third period, Phoenix erased the eight point deficit and led 67-65.

At the outset of the fourth quarter, the Warriors mounted one last drive. They tied the game at seventy, but Phoenix countered with an 8-2 run and never trailed again. The final score was 94-86, giving the Suns the Western Conference Championship and a shot at a world title. They did it behind a patient offense and a smothering defense which held Barry to only six points in the second half.

"As the game wound down to the final minutes, Rick's frustration with his teammates became apparent," Dick recalls. "Rick is the type of player who always wanted the ball in his hands when the chips were down. We worked very hard to stop his teammates from getting him the ball. I thought we did an outstanding job of shutting both him and Charlie (Johnson) down."

"We've been trying like heck to gain some respectability," an elated MacLeod told Dave Hicks of the

Arizona Republic at the post-game press conference. "A lot of people have laughed at us, and there haven't been many nice things said about us. But I don't care what they say now. We're one of only two teams left. We got here behind the work of guys who have worked their fannies off---great guys, intelligent men. We've come a long way."

"I just can't believe it," exclaimed a proud and humble Jerry Colangelo. "All I did the whole game was pray. When it came down to the end and we won it, I just thanked God."

The Suns' 94-86 upset over Golden State in Oakland left the Warrior dynasty in shambles and sent Phoenix into the NBA finals against the Boston Celtics. When the team flew home to Phoenix, thousands of well-wishers converged on the airport to meet them.

"Coming home to all of those fans was incredible," Dick recalls. "That was one of the most exciting days of my life. Tom and several friends had flown up to Oakland to see the final game and we celebrated together at the hotel for awhile. When we got back to Phoenix the terminal was wall-to-wall people; it took us well over an hour to get through the place. By the time I finally got home I was physically exhausted, but my mind was still racing."

"Watching the Suns win the conference final against Golden State was special, but I saw something after the game that for me was much more poignant," Bill Shover recalls. "I went up to the hotel room where the team was celebrating and saw Dick and Tom sitting side by side on a bed talking to their mother on the phone. They both had tears in their eyes. As I watched them I could not help but remember that state final loss against Kokomo. I thought it was a testimony to their character that even though Tom was not a member of the team he and Dick were sharing this moment as though it were something that they both had accomplished. The more I thought about it, the more I realized that it was indeed an accomplishment to which they had both contributed."

* *

The NBA finals pitted one of the league's up and coming franchises against "the" franchise. While the Suns were enjoying their first trip ever to the finals, the Celtics had been to the finals more years than their opponents had been fielding teams. And the 1975-76 version of "the Green" featured several of the Celtics all-time greats. Paul Silas, John Havlicek, Don Nelson, Dave Cowens, and Jo Jo White anchored this team of veteran performers.

The finals opened in Boston where the Celtics quickly established that this was to be a physical series with plenty of punishing picks and rough fouls. With Cowens, Nelson, and Silas underneath, they planned to contest every shot and fight for every rebound. On the strength of solid performances from all their veterans, Boston won the opening game 98-87. Dave Cowens and Jo Jo White led the scoring for the victors with twenty-five and twenty-two points respectively, while Alvan Adams led all scorers with twenty-six points.

"Alvan had a fantastic year for us," Dick explains. "He had played for Macleod at Oklahoma. He left school a year early and when we used our first pick to get him, I wondered if we'd done the right thing," Dick recalls. "Alvan had lost some weight on account of a virus and when he showed up for training camp he was all skin and bones.

"He was only 6'9" which is small for a center and, as skinny as he was, I figured he'd get pushed around quite a bit. But when he started playing, I soon realized that he was a talent. Alvan was extremely athletic. He was quick and could jump. He also had excellent passing skills and could hit the outside jumper. Macleod's offense required a good passing center, so Alvan fit right in.

"By the end of the season, Alvan had become one of the most dominating players in our conference. He handled Golden State's big men with surprising ease and against Boston he was giving (Dave) Cowens and Ard (Jim Ard, the Celtics' backup center) all they could handle."

In the second game, Boston carried a slim five-point lead at the half and then chased the Suns right out of the building. The Celtics outscored Phoenix 34-16 in the third period and led by as many as twenty-eight points in a 105-90 rout that left Phoenix wondering what hit them.

The bulk of what hit them came off the bench in the person of John Havlicek who scored twenty-three points. "When we have Havlicek in there we can press and run," Boston coach Tommy Heinsohn told the press after the game. "And, as soon as we start running, good things begin to happen." In addition to Havlicek's effort, Paul Silas grabbed seventeen rebounds and made several critical steals. The former Celtic, Paul Westphal, led the stunned Suns with twenty-eight points and Alvan Adams contributed nineteen.

After two games in Boston, the series headed to Phoenix for game three---and not a moment too soon for the Suns. "We'd won seventeen of our last eighteen homes games, and despite the big loss, we were still confident that we could beat them," Dick recalls. "We figured that if we could win all the games in our building all we would need to do is to `steal' one in the Garden. "They were as physical a team as we'd played all season. And Havlicek was something else. They just wound him up and put him on the floor. He wasn't spectacular; he'd just go and go and go. John could play all day and he seldom made mistakes."

In front of a capacity crowd at Veterans Memorial Coliseum, The Suns showed Boston how they had won the West by beating the Celtics 105-98. Phoenix led by fifteen points early in the fourth and then withstood a ferocious Celtic comeback. Alvan Adams again led the way for the victors with thirty-three points and a dozen blocked shots.

Game four, also played in Phoenix, was decided during the last thirteen seconds of play. The Suns led 109-107 and Boston had the ball. After calling a timeout, the Celtics worked a play to get the ball into the hands of Jo Jo White. White, working against Ricky Sobers, had to settle for a twenty-foot jumper which rattled off the rim, tieing the series at two.

"We felt pretty good going back into Boston," Dick recalls. "We'd won the games on our court. All we had to do was steal this next one at the Garden and then win another one at home. I think we all felt it was a possibility."

"Even when they tied the series at two, we weren't the least bit worried," responds John Havlicek. "Phoenix had a solid team, but we thought we were a lot better than them. In the two games we'd lost, the scores had been close and it never even entered into our thinking that the Suns could beat us in our building. We went back to Boston thinking that we had two more games to win."

The fifth game of the series will always be remembered as one of the greatest professional basketball games ever played. Game five featured incredible clutch shooting by both teams and three overtimes, but at the outset it looked as though Boston would win in a rout. Midway through the second period the Celtics held a 42-20 advantage. But by late in the fourth period Phoenix had erased that twenty-two point deficit and with twenty-three seconds left, they led 95-94.

With time running out, John Havlicek, who was playing on a bad foot, drove to the basket and was fouled. "Hondo" hit the first of his two free throws to tie the game, but missed the second, sending the game into overtime.

The overtime period saw the Celtics move out to a four point advantage. But Phoenix came back as Gar Heard hit a jumper late in the overtime to tie the game at 101, forcing yet another overtime.

In the second overtime, it was Phoenix who nudged ahead. They led 110-109 with only seven seconds left. But Boston's superman, John Havlicek weaved his way down to the other end and with :01 showing on the clock he hit a lean-in bank shot that put his team up 111-110.

"As soon as I saw that the shot went in I got the heck off of the floor and headed for the locker room," John explains. "I love Celtic fans, they are the greatest fans in the world, but when they are in frenzy such as they were that night its best to run and hide. One year I had my jersey ripped clean off of my body and had to start punching people to save myself from being trampled and seriously hurt.

"Anyway, most of us were down in the locker room thinking that we had won when someone came in said there was still one second left on the clock. We put our jerseys back on and went back up to the floor. The place was in complete bedlam. Fans were running everywhere. I heard they even tried to beat up a referee. It was wild out there that night."

"Wild is putting it mildly," Dick interjects. "That organization would do almost anything to intimidate an opponent and that night was a good example. They did not have near enough security to handle that mob. And when the fans did start running out on the floor, the few security people there didn't do much to stop them. It was scary. All of those people were coming down on us, shouting and becoming violent. They beat up the Richie Powers (the ref), which was a little ironic because Richie had failed to give Paul Silas a technical foul when he asked for a timeout when the Celtics had no timeouts left. If he would have made that call, we probably would have won in regulation." (Powers later explained that he did not make that call because he didn't feel the game should have been decided by the referee.)

When order was finally restored, the Suns faced a terrific dilemma. They trailed by one point and had but one second to score a basket. If they'd had a timeout to call they would get the ball at half court, but without it they had to work from baseline to baseline. As Paul Westphal received the ball from the referee to trigger that final play, he took a gamble. Paul turned to the ref and asked for a timeout.

This move would cost the Suns a technical foul, which Jo Jo White hit to give the Celtics a 112-110 lead, but Phoenix now had the ball at half court. "During the timeout I reminded Heinsohn that we still had one foul to give," explains Paul Silas. "I suggested that we foul the first guy who touched the ball, but Tommy disagreed. He doubted that anyone could hit a basket in one second."

However, when the Suns came back out the floor this is exactly what they did. Curtis Perry, assigned the task of throwing the ball inbounds, found Gar Heard at the top of the key. Heard caught the ball, turned against Don Nelson and fired a lofting jumpshot that hit nothing but net.

"It felt good all the way," Heard would later tell an amazed and exhausted press corp. "As soon as it left my hands I knew it was two." Heard's shot brought the rowdy Boston crowd to its feet and then quietly sat them down. For the first time in the history of the NBA Finals, a game was headed for a third overtime.

In the third overtime an unlikely hero emerged. Glenn McDonald, a second year guard from Long Beach State, scored six points for the Celtics as they finally built a lead the rough and tumble Suns could not surmount. Boston pulled ahead 124-118 and then held on to win 128-126.

The aftermath of the contest brought a flood of praise for the participants and a deluge of disbelief over the behavior of the Celtic fans. "You cannot imagine how difficult it is to try and listen to the coach when fans are standing right behind you shouting obscenities and spitting on you," Dick insists. "And throughout the game I never heard anyone get on the public address system and say anything to try and keep things under control."

"That was a difficult loss to swallow," he adds. "Our guys played their butts off for sixty-three minutes and we came away empty."

The emotionally drained Suns, now trailing three games to two, headed back to Phoenix for game six. The team travelled home on Saturday and then had to play again at 12:30 in the afternoon on Sunday. "Losing in three overtimes, then travelling two-thousand miles and having to play again within twenty-four hours was a tremendous challenge," recalls Gar Heard.

Unfortunately, the Suns were not quite up to the challenge. In game six, in front of a packed Coliseum, the Celtics showed the poise for which they were famous and ended Phoenix's Cinderella story with an 87-80 victory.

"We were a little flat," Dick admits. "The triple

overtime was still in our minds and we didn't generate the type of intensity we needed to beat a great team. You have to give John, Don, Jo Jo, Paul and the rest of the Celtics a lot of credit. They played excellent ball every game and in the end we fell a little short.

"Even so, winning our conference and then playing for the world championship was the greatest thrill of my entire basketball career. Every once in awhile I'll catch myself thinking about those series with Golden State and Boston. The memories bring a smile to my face."

Dick congratulates John Havlicek after game six of the 1976 world championship. (Photo courtesy of The Arizona Republic)

*Tom in his rookie
season in Detroit.*

(Photo by Albert Barg)

*Rick Barry tries a
shot against Dick.
during their rookie
season.*

*(Photo by George
Kalinsky)*

Dick as a Knick.
(Photo courtesy of Dick Van Arsdale)

*(Photo by Sue Levy.
Courtesy of the Arizona
Republic)*

*(Photo courtesy of the
Phoenix Suns.)*

(Photos Courtesy of Tom Van Arsdale)

Tom as a Sixer.

(Photos by Ed Butler.)

(Photos by Roy Molen. Courtesy of the Arizona Republic.)

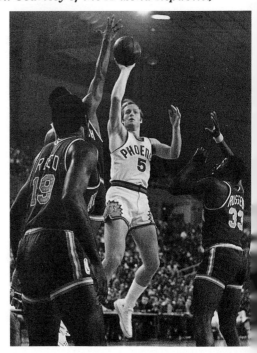

(Photos courtesy of Dick Van Arsdale.)

Tom and his family: Kathy, Kerrie, Amy, and Chris.

(Photos courtesy of Dick Van Arsdale.)

Tom as a Sun.

Chapter 10

Tom tries to pass around Dick in a game in Atlanta.
(Photo courtesy of Tom Van Arsdale)

Throughout their NBA careers, Dick and Tom amassed amazingly similar statistics. Both averaged thirty-four minutes per game and in those thirty-four minutes Dick averaged sixteen points to Tom's fifteen. Dick dished out an average of three assists per game while Tom averaged three, and each could be expected to accumulate an average of three fouls per contest. Tom and Dick were each named team captain in the same season. Both were first team all rookie in their first season and both were named to three All-Star squads.

The twins are as close in the statistic book as any two players have ever been, yet their NBA careers took on two completely different personalities. While Dick spent all but three seasons with the Suns in Phoenix, Tom would eventually play in six cities. Dick played in three playoffs, including the 1975-76 NBA finals. Tom was never on a team that made the playoffs. In fact, Tom never finished a season with a team that had better than a .500 record.

"That is one of the more bitter ironies about professional sports," offers Cotton Fitzsimmons regarding the twins similar statistics and dissimilar situations. "I suppose that in some instances you would say that one or the other had more heart or was somehow doing something better. But this was not the case with Dick and Tom. They both brought the same type of attitudes and abilities to every game. I coached them both and I know. They both gave 110 percent every time they were out on the floor."

While there were contrasts in Tom and Dick's NBA careers there were contrasts in their private lives as well. Dick had dated Barbara all through college and married her shortly after graduating. Not long after that they started their family. Tom, on the other hand, dated for a few years after graduating. He then married Jeanne Klise whom he had met through his old college teammate Jimmy Rayl. Unfortunately, this marriage did not last.

"When Dick married Barb, I remember feeling a little lost. I wasn't envious of him, but I felt there was something missing in my life," Tom explains. "Shortly after their wedding Jimmy introduced me to Jeannie. We dated for a year, and then decided to get married. In retrospect, that was obviously a bad decision. I didn't want to be alone, but Jeannie and I weren't right for each other.

"I suppose that somewhere deep in my heart I knew that I was making a terrible mistake. But at that time in my life, I had yet to learn to stop and take the time to fathom my heart's deepest desires. I was only interested in what was going on at the surface.

"Our marriage lasted about three years. We had some good times, but our goals and attitudes grew in other directions. I started doubting about our future and began to focus on what was best for me instead of us. The final months of that relationship were a learning experience.

"The divorce was final the same summer the team moved from Cincinnati to Kansas City. I moved to Phoenix that summer. And as I grew acquainted with my new home, I spent time thinking about my life and the mistakes I'd made. I knew I did not want to live alone and that I wanted to be married and to have a family. But I also realized that I would have to find the right woman.

"I started going to church at this time, too. My relationship with God had never been close. And, as I sat there Sunday after Sunday, I also began to realize that God had an important role to play in my life. I decided to let him play that role, and soon after making that decision, I could just feel that I was going to be all right.

"Late that summer, before heading to training camp, several friends fixed me up with a date. The young lady's name was Kathy Wilmanns. Since our first date was a casual event with many other people, we didn't talk much. After the date I wasn't sure at all that she liked me or that I liked her.

"I left for training camp and returned several times over the course of the year, but I didn't see Kathy. Then, after a disastrous season where I'd been traded by Kansas City to Philly, I came home to Phoenix and ended up going out on another date with Kathy."

"We went out alone this time," Kathy recalls, picking up the story. "The first time we'd gone out the people we were with had him talking about professional basketball. I was not a sports fan and didn't know much at all about basketball. I had nothing to say or ask about the game and what Tom had said about it wasn't all that interesting to me.

"When we went out alone, it was different. We talked about everything under the sun---and a little bit about basketball. After that date, I was a little more impressed with Tom Van Arsdale."

"And I was totally taken by her," says Tom. "During the rest of the summer, I tried to see her as much as I could. And along the way, I kept asking myself: `Is this the woman with whom I wish to spend the rest of my life.'

"The answer was yes and I began to look at the situation in terms of the long run. I thought about the responsibilities of marriage and of becoming a parent. It's probably a good thing she didn't know about all of the thinking that was going on in my head. If she had, she might have run off."

"I'll never forget his proposal," Kathy interjects. "It

was early in the summer and we were driving home from a date. Tom was due to head back to training camp in two months and on this particular night he had been rather quiet. I could tell he was thinking about something, but I didn't know what. We were driving along in silence and suddenly he turned to me and said: `Kathy, I've been thinking about going back to Philadelphia. I'll miss you. I love you and I want to marry you."

Kathy and Tom were married several weeks later and then moved to Philadelphia for Tom's first full season with the team. For Tom this marriage meant a second chance to be a husband and a father. For Kathy, it meant leaving sunny Phoenix for a long winter and spring in the city of brotherly love.

"Well, we said for better or for worse. And the worse came right away," Kathy laughs. "I'm certain that Philadelphia is a wonderful town, but our first winter there was awful. All I remember is cold weather.

"We moved there during the gas crunch of the early seventies and one of my scarier memories involved driving around a snowy and cold south Philadelphia with my fuel gauge on empty, looking for a gas station that still had gas.

"We rented furniture and moved it into a dingy brownstone in the Germantown area. Our apartment was nice, but not at all like our home in Phoenix. Tom was on the road a lot, and that, too, was something that I'd expected, but never grew accustomed to. Of course, I realized that our lives would not always be this way and I had Phoenix to look forward to for the holidays and after the season. But for a new bride who didn't know much at all about her husband's profession, I often felt like someone standing on the outside looking in."

* *

On December 23, 1973 Tom and Dick received the news that their father had died. Raymond Van Arsdale had suffered from a long illness and the twins describe his death as a blessing to both him and his family. "By the time dad died he'd been in and out of hospitals for ten years," Tom recalls. "In the later years, he required quite a bit of help and it got to the point where mom was no longer able to manage. Then we had to have him put into a nursing home."

"Van was never the same after Manual lost that state championship game," Hilda recalls. "His whole life had been built around seeing those boys win a state championship. When they lost he was devastated and I don't think he ever got over it. In the years after that he suffered from depression and his health began to fail in general."

"While its true that the last years of dad's life were difficult years for all of us, we will always remember him as a devoted father," Dick adds. "I cannot imagine any father being as devoted to his sons as dad was to us. When we were children, he took us with him everywhere he went and he always encouraged us to do our very best."

"During those years of his illness, we also discovered that our mother is a tower of strength," Tom interjects. "She had always been a strong person, but watching her deal with the various problems that came along as a result of dad's extended illness gave us a deeper admiration for the depth of her character.

"In those years during which dad's health began to deteriorate, our hearts went out to both him and mom. They'd given us such a wonderful childhood and it was most unfortunate that they had to suffer during these golden years of their life."

* *

When Tom had been traded by Kansas City to Philadelphia, he had made up his mind that he would go to Philadelphia and help that team turn things around. During the 1973-74 season he did just that. Tom and his Sixer teammates won eighteen more games then they had during the previous season.

Tom, now in his ninth year, carried a 19.6 scoring average, only a point off the clip of the team's leading scorer, Fred Carter. "I don't know why Kansas City ever let him go," remarks Tom's former Sixer teammate and road roommate Steve Mix. "Tom brought enthusiasm and tenacity to every game. When you lose as much as we did, it is difficult to always be `up' for games, but somehow Tom managed to do it. His attitude was contagious and I think he played a big role in helping improve the team's won-lost record."

"I was pleased with my year," Tom recalls. "And the team, too, despite our losing record, had taken giant steps towards becoming a contender. I was pleased to be a part of that turnaround, but I still would have much preferred to be playing in Phoenix.

"We went home for the summer and, as the time for training camp approached, I could tell that Kathy was dreading another eight months in Philadelphia. I think we both had begun to look forward to the time when I would be able to spend more time with her and Kerrie (their baby daughter).

"I still enjoyed playing the game, but I also saw that my career was going to end in a few years. When I played in Cincinnati, I had put looking for a post-basketball career on the back burner. Back then I spent my summers visiting basketball camps, trying to give something back to the game. I also had an annual obligation to the Indiana Air National Guard which ended in 1972. With my entire summer free of any obligations and a family to think about, I started looking around for something I might like to do after I got out of basketball. That something turned out to be real estate.

"Dick and I both got involved at the same time. We worked for George Moerkerke and Bill Howard, a transplanted Hoosier. They taught us about the business and, of course, there were courses to take and licensing tests. We did all of those things and the more involved we got, the more we liked it. Real estate was a challenging field and Arizona---especially the Phoenix area---was in the midst of unprecedented growth. As Kathy, Kerrie, and I headed back to Philadelphia, I was eager to start another basketball season, but in the back of my mind I was making plans for the rest of my life. It was an exciting time for me because I was looking at where I was going, not just at where I was or where I'd been."

Tom's third season in Philadelphia lasted only nine games. Several days before Christmas, the 76ers traded him to Atlanta for Clyde Lee. "It wasn't much of a Christmas present," Tom laughs. "But we weren't too disappointed. I had a feeling that this was going to happen. You never know where you're going to go, you just know that you're going."

"I was happy to get out of Philadelphia," Kathy recalls. "I figured Atlanta would be a little warmer. We went home to Phoenix for the holidays and then Tom arranged to have our things moved from Philadelphia to Atlanta. We lived in a hotel for a couple of weeks and then got an apartment. I had been accustomed to a more stable lifestyle and a move like this threw me off a bit. When I look back at those hectic times, I wish I'd had a better attitude. I knew that our future would not be as helter-skelter as it was when Tom was playing, but I didn't always see it that way in the heat of the moment."

"I disagree with her," says Tom. "She did a great job. I did not like having to move around as much as we did. Living in a hotel for weeks at a time or an apartment for half-a-year was not my idea of the best environment for my family. But basketball was my life and I think Kathy did a wonderful job of realizing this and accepting the inconveniences that went along with it."

Tom's move to Atlanta found him playing for Cotton Fitzsimmons, who'd previously coached Dick in Phoenix. "Being able to play for Cotton was definitely a plus," Tom admits. "Cotton made playing basketball a lot of fun because he was always positive. He had so much enthusiasm and he was fiercely loyal to his players. You didn't have to be around him very long before you knew that he was going to be one of the greatest NBA coaches ever."

Tom stepped into Cotton's starting lineup and led the team in scoring. "I've always said if you've seen one Van Arsdale, you've seen them all," Cotton contests. "Tommy was exactly the same type of ball player as his brother. I loved coaching them. You could use them as an example for your other players. If a guy came to me pouting because he wasn't getting enough playing time I could point to Dick or Tom and say: Look at Van Arsdale out there. Is he whining about his minutes? No, they'd answer, of course he's not complaining about his minutes, you play him all the time coach. That's right, I'd tell them. I play him all the time and you know why? And, of course they knew why--- because Van Arsdale, Dick or Tom, was giving all he had the whole time he was on the floor. If all of my players had played with the intensity of the Van Arsdales, then I'd have a fist full of championship rings."

In addition to Tom, the Hawks featured Lou Hudson and sensational rookie guard, John Drew. "The first time I played with John I knew he was going to become a great player," Tom recalls. "I had played with Nate Archibald and Norm Van Lier, Johnny Drew came from that same mold. He was quick, had an excellent outside shot, and was one of the best offensive rebounders I'd ever seen."

Despite the additions of Tom Van Arsdale and John Drew, Atlanta finished the 1974-75 season with a 31-51 record, and, for the tenth year in a row, Tom watched the playoffs from the sideline. "What can I say? It was tough. It is hard to imagine that anyone could play for four different teams over ten years and never make the playoffs---but it happens. It happened to me. All I could do was look forward to the next season and hope that my team would play better. I tried to stay positive, and it wasn't always easy."

* *

In Tom's second season with the Hawks, his scoring average fell by nearly eight points and his playing time dwindled. "I suppose that the '75-76 season was a bit of an unpleasant reminder that I was getting older and that it was time to start thinking about what I planned to do with the rest of my life. Things might have been different if I'd stayed with a team for more than several years. I think a franchise tends to be a little more loyal to older players who have been with the team for many years. But I was certainly not the heart and soul of the Atlanta franchise and by season's end I had my suspicions that Atlanta just might try to ship me somewhere else.

"By this time I wanted nothing more than to enjoy at least one season playing with Dick. And when I say that,

I don't mean it in the sense that I was tired of basketball or that I felt something was owed to me. I just wanted to spend a season in Phoenix.

"When the season ended, the Hawks fired Cotton, making me even more certain that I was not going to be a member of the team in '76-77. Sure enough, I got the call and the news was that I'd been traded to Buffalo.

"When Buffalo's trainer called and asked what number I wanted on my uniform, I told him I wasn't going to come to Buffalo and that they'd better make a deal with Phoenix or I was going to retire. Several weeks passed and then the trainer called me again, asking what number I wanted. I said: `Maybe you didn't hear me right the first time. I'm not coming to Buffalo. Make a deal with Phoenix or I'll retire. Shortly after that Jerry Colangelo called and said that Buffalo wanted to deal me to the Suns. Jerry wanted me, but he said I'd have to take a cut in pay. I gladly agreed."

"I'd been trying to make a deal for Tom almost since the day the franchise was born," explains Jerry. "I almost had it done a couple of times, but then Tom would have a great couple of games or something else would come up and the deals just didn't go through. When he was with Cincinnati, we had a deal ready to go: then Tom went out and scored forty points and Cincinnati decided they didn't want to get rid of him.

"We tried to get him when Kansas City was shopping him around. In fact, I went to Kansas City to close that deal, but when I got to the meeting they wanted to turn the thing around: they wanted Dick. I told them I'd never let Dick go and by the time it was all said and done I'd have Tom too."

"I was excited that he and I were going to have a chance to play together, but it really happened too late," explains Dick. "We were both in the later stages of our careers. On the other hand, I suppose we were better off by not being on the same team all those years because that would have meant that he and I would be in competition for playing time. It could have hurt us both.

"There had been rumors of a possible trade for as long as we were in the league. Red Kerr once told me that we'd made a trade for Tom, but when I asked him who we had to give up he said: `you.' Every once in awhile I'd hear about a possible deal, but it never happened until Tom told Buffalo he was going to retire."

Tom's first season in Phoenix turned out to be the last in his career. "I enjoyed that year because Dick and I were able to play together again, but by mid-season I decided that I would retire at the end of the year.

"I'd been spending more time on the bench than ever before and my thoughts were turning more towards my family and what I would do after basketball. I did not want to be the type of player who just hangs on from year to year until he retires because no one will pick him up off the waiver wire either. In the end I was able to walk away from the game with only one regret---I never made it to the playoffs.

"We had gone to the NBA Finals the year before Tom arrived and I figured we'd at least make the playoffs that next season," Dick recalls. "Unfortunately, our front line got hit with a bunch of injuries. Alvan Adams, Curtis Perry, and Gar Heard all missed at least half of the season. Without them we didn't stand a chance at making the playoffs. I was disappointed for the team---but especially disappointed for Tom.

"When it came time for Tom to play in his last professional basketball game, I tried to get him to do something that we had never done in the entire time we'd been playing basketball. I asked him to switch jerseys with me."

"But I didn't," Tom interjects. "At the time I thought it would be trivializing what we'd been doing for twelve years, but in retrospect I wish I had."

* *

Tom spent his first summer away from basketball building his real estate business and adjusting to the notion that in October he would not be joining a team for training camp.

"Away from basketball, I enjoyed the challenges in my work in real estate. I felt I might have a future in that field and I was eager to get started at it full time. When I retired and watched the opening of another NBA season, however, it bothered me that I was no longer going to be out on the playing floor, listening to the cheers from the crowd and competing with the greatest athletes in the world. I was a little depressed. I had enjoyed the life of a celebrity and I missed the comraderie of my teammates. For twenty-four years basketball had been the driving force in my life and being away from it required a complete change in my way of thinking."

Despite some initial concerns and disappointments, Tom made a successful transition from playing in front of crowds on a basketball court to completing paperwork from behind a desk.

"When we're told that professional athletes rise to prominence because of their dedication and hard work, we sometimes forget that this is the same way that people rise to the top of other professions," explains Bill Howard, Tom's first employer in the real estate business. "Tom Van Arsdale is a classic example of this, both as a ball player and as a real estate broker. With his celebrity status, he would not have had to work as hard as some of my other people, but he worked harder. Tom approached his business interests with the same tenacity that he'd formerly used to track down loose balls.

"Often times an employer will take on a celebrity simply for the promotion potential of saying I've got so-and-so working for me. In many instances that celebrity isn't worth a hoot in the business climate. He or she is just there to look good. But such was never the case with Tom and Dick. They always carried their share of the workload."

"These are nice things for Bill to say," says Tom, "but he is far too modest. Bill Howard taught Dick and me everything we know about the real estate business. And, while it is true that we've had to earn our way in basketball, business, and in life, we have also had tremendous support all the way. Our parents gave us a wonderful foundation of ethics and values; our coaches were patient teachers, who unselfishly gave of their time to see that we would succeed; and our mentors, business people such as Bill Howard, have taught us the many facets of our various business interests---all of which has led to our success. I'm grateful to so many people who helped along the way.

As the years pass, Tom continues to enjoy his family, his work, and basketball. "Basketball is no longer the most important thing in my life," he confesses, "but it is still very dear to me. In the days of my youth, I spent twenty-four years playing basketball. Those years created a wealth of fond memories. But it does not compare to the joy I now share with Kathy, Kerrie, Chris, and Amy (the youngest of Tom and Kathy's children born in 1981). The pleasures I now enjoy seem to bring a deeper contentment."

Chapter 11

Dick (left) and Tom (right) Van Arsdale golfing in Paradise.

The 1976-77 NBA season was the last for both Tom and Dick. However, while Tom's retirement had been planned, Dick's had not. At the conclusion of the '76-77 season Dick had presumed he would be back for his tenth season with the Suns. But at a quiet post-season breakfast meeting with head coach John MacLeod, Dick discovered that the coach's plans for the team did not include him.

"I was as shocked as I had been on the day that I became a Sun," Dick recalls. "I had played out the last year of my contract and before I went to Jerry to negotiate another one I wanted to meet with John to get a sense of where he was taking the team. I understood that I would no longer be starting and that whatever role I had would be limited, but I had no idea that John would suggest I retire.

"I went to Jerry about it and he supported John, adding that I had a place with the team for as long as I wanted one. I talked to Barb and Tom about it and finally made the decision that it would be best for the Suns if I stepped aside.

"I can't say that it was easy. I'd come to the franchise during its first year and had grown with the team and its fans. I just didn't know how I would be able to watch a Phoenix Suns basketball game without having the opportunity to effect the outcome. I would miss playing for the team and I would miss the competition. I suppose I could have made a fuss about it and ended up somewhere else for a season or two, but I could not imagine leaving Phoenix.

"Fortunately, Tom and I had been involved in real estate for a couple of years and it looked like I could make a future in that field. When I let Jerry know my decision, the Suns made a deal with me to do the color commentary for their games. The situation with which I was presented was not a bad situation, but I still hated the fact that I would not be involved as a player.

Dick announced his retirement at a luncheon at the Phoenix Country Club. "I was there," recalls Bill Shover. "It was the silliest thing I'd ever seen. At the time, Dick was one of the few Suns who played defense and they needed him for that more than ever. As I walked out of the building that day, I was feeling pretty low for Dick and marvelling at the Suns' stupidity when I ran across Proski (Joe Proski has been the Suns' trainer since 1968). He gave me a disgusted look and poked his thumb back at the building. 'Isn't that a crock of shit,' he said. 'Now who the hell have we got to play any defense?' And if you don't think Joe knew what he was talking about, it wasn't long after that they asked Dick to come out of retirement to play."

"I had a difficult decision to make," explains MacLeod. "The team needed a few changes, and with the personnel moves we were planning to make, Dick was not going to be getting as many minutes. I'd be the first to say that he was among the finest players I have ever coached. But his best days were behind him and I thought this was an opportunity for him to go out while he was still close to the top."

"Of course, Dick Van Arsdale could have played for another year or two," Jerry Colangelo adds. "But Dick had never been the type of player who liked to spend a lot of time on the bench. Had he stayed on as a player this would have been the situation he faced. I think he made the right choice (by retiring). His commitment to this club over the years has been complete and I've always appreciated the effort he has given. As soon as he decided that he wanted to retire, I let him know that he had a place with this team for as long as he wanted one."

"If you wanted an example of what type of person Dick Van Arsdale is, just look at the way he handled being forced to retire," Joe Gilmartin offers. "Dick could have fought it; I'm sure that some other team in the league would have loved to have him. But he didn't fight it. He didn't fight because he felt a loyalty towards Phoenix and the Suns' organization. And he didn't fight it because he is not stupid. I think Dick realized that in the long run he was doing what was best for all the parties involved---including himself."

"If Joe said that he must be right, because those sports journalists are never wrong," Dick laughs. "I guess I did do what was best for me. By the time I had that meeting with John, I had been involved in real estate for several years and I enjoyed it. I had that to turn to and then Jerry promised that I could stay with the team in some capacity. I ended up working as the color commentator with Al McCoy. Doing the broadcasts kept me in front of the fans and I think staying in the public eye helped my business interests as well as permitting me to continue to be a part of the Suns' organization. Even so, leaving the game was one of the toughest things I've ever done.

In October of 1977, the Suns and their fans honored Dick Van Arsdale with a retirement party at a home game. "Jerry flew my mother and other members of my family into town," Dick recalls. "That evening was one of the most special in my life. I had always tried to do my best on the basketball court and the fans in Phoenix rewarded me well. I'll never forget the way they got behind the new franchise and cheered us---even those small crowds from way back in the beginning.

"To have played in such a great situation for nine years and then to be honored by having my number retired was a humbling feeling. As I stood out there, I could not help but think of all of the wonderful people who had supported me along the way."

After Dick retired he stayed with the team, working as a color commentator alongside Al McCoy, "the voice of the Suns."

"I have always thought Dick was a class act," remarks McCoy. "And I thought he was especially classy in the way he handled that retirement business. When I heard he and I would be working together, I thought that was a great idea. He'd had experience in television and then when he came on line he was eager to learn, he was always looking for ways to improve.

"We worked together for fifteen years and over that time I've come to know him a consummate professional. He comes to the broadcast booth as well prepared as he did the playing floor."

In addition to his work in broadcasting Suns' games, Dick continued to work in real estate. After his retirement he and Tom decided to go into business for themselves. "This had been a goal of ours for quite some time," Tom explains. "We wanted to see if we could create a business and make it grow. When we started Van Arsdale Properties Incorporated, our plan was for slow growth in an organized manner. We kept our overhead low by doing as much of the work as we could. In the beginning, we answered our own phones, made cold calls, did research, and even typed our own letters and contracts."

"We knew that our celebrity status as basketball players would open a few doors, but once inside those doors we understood we would have to show our clients that we knew what we were talking about," Dick adds. "We built our business on our credibility as real estate brokers, not on the fact that we were once professional basketball players."

Ron Haarer, an Arizona real estate developer who has done quite a bit of business with Dick and Tom, explains what Dick and Tom have done for him in the real estate business. "My dealings with Dick and Tom have been in the area of 'master planned communities.' A master plan community begins with a large piece of land, which is then parcelled off into tracts to be sold as residential housing, apartments, strip malls, and so on. These communities are usually developed around a recreational facility such as a golf course. Dick and Tom helped sell these tracts to builders or investment consortiums. Their income came from the commissions generated by each sale.

"When Dick and Tom got involved with a project it usually went well. I remember one instance when they sold out an entire community within a few months. Their celebrity status certainly helped, but they were also the type of business people who tried to see that deals were made on the basis that everybody wins. I have seen them be more than fair with clients and their approach has always been to place their integrity before profits.

"The twins would also form their own limited partnerships to invest in different tracts. It made me feel good to know that they thought so highly of the various projects that they were willing to invest their own money. Over the years, I've come to know them as savvy businessmen who are honest and loyal."

Within five years, Van Arsdale Properties grew to the point where Dick and Tom took on a partner. "In the beginning we imagined that both of us would be able to handle everything that came along, but after a few years we discovered that we could use someone who had a better understanding of banking," Tom explains. "In 1982 we brought Butch Joyner in as a partner. He'd been working in the banking industry, and thus was able to fit right in. Butch had played for Lou Watson's 1967 Big Ten championship team and we had known him when he was a freshman at IU. In fact, Butch would have played with us when he was a sophomore, but I fell on his foot and broke it. He missed the entire season because of that."

"Aside from that business about my destroyed basketball career, Dick and Tom have been two of my best friends. It was a privilege to work with them," says Butch. "They worked as hard at making their business successful as they had on the basketball court. The only thing I didn't like about being a partner was that I was always out-voted two to one. Try as I might, I could never get one or the other of those guys to vote with me."

"If Butch had ever been right about anything, I would have sided with him," Tom jokes. On a more serious note he adds, "Butch brought an important dimension to our business. With him around, we were able to better understand the intricacies of real estate finance. The government was constantly changing the rules and banks, too, made it difficult for anyone other than an expert to understand real estate financing. Butch had a background in finance so we felt he gave us an advantage over some of our competitors."

"He was a great sales person, too," adds Dick. "Butch shared our attitude about making deals wherein everyone is a winner."

In 1986 the federal government passed a tax reform act that drastically changed the rules regarding taxes and real estate investment. This change in rules, combined with a general downturn in the real estate market, had a devastating effect on the real estate business in Arizona. Among the catastrophic results was the failure of many banks whose loan portfolios were replete with bad loans on over-valued real estate. In the following years, fortunes were lost, lives ruined, and the real estate market fell into a steep descent.

"Our business was not immune," Tom recalls. "But we'd kept our overhead low and, while other people in real estate had leveraged themselves to the hilt, we did not have much debt."

"We understood that the rewards for the big investment were greater, but we also knew that the risks were greater, too," adds Dick. "Tom and I had always been willing to let other people go for the big rewards by taking big risks. Which is not to say that we didn't have our share of losses; I don't think anybody in the business out here escaped unscathed."

As fate would have it, several events took place in 1986---events that would lead Dick away from his real estate business and back into basketball.

The 1986-87 Phoenix Suns got off to a terrible start. The team had been shook by a drug scandal and floundered near the bottom of the standings. The Suns' poor performance caused the management to decide that it was time to make a coaching change. John MacLeod, who had been with the team for thirteen years, was dismissed, and Dick Van Arsdale was asked to take over.

"Jerry asked me to come over to his house one night, so I figured something was up, but I had no idea what," Dick recalls. "He told me that the owners wanted to make a coaching change and then asked if I would coach the team for the remainder of the season. I agreed, but with the understanding that I had no desire to be a head coach in the NBA for any more than the remainder of the season.

I took the job because I saw it as an opportunity for me to give something back to the franchise."

When MacLeod left the team had an 22-34 record. Under Dick's guidance, the team ended the season winning ten of their last eleven games. In his twenty-six game tenure, he coached the Suns to a 14-12 record. In 1987 John Wetzel replaced Dick as coach, but Dick continued to see his role with the team expand.

"In 1987 the owners put the team up for sale and Jerry decided to buy it," Dick recalls. "He asked me to invest, which I did, and he also asked me to work in in the front office in addition to doing the color commentary. The real estate market started going sour at about the same time that Jerry offered me an opportunity. In that respect, the timing was perfect.

"This team has been a part of my life now for over twenty years. I feel the same loyalty to the Suns that a twenty-year career executive might feel towards a corporation. This franchise has given so much to me and I feel lucky to have the opportunity to give something back."

At the end of the 1991-92 season, the Suns moved into the America West Arena. The new stadium, which seats 19500, was made possible through the strong support of Suns' fans who have stayed with the team through thick and thin. 1991-92 also marked the retirement of Cotton Fitzsimmons, who had come back to the team in 1988. In his most recent tenure as head coach, Cotton has led the team to four consecutive fifty-plus victory seasons. He has retired to the front office, assuming the color commentary duties from Dick. Dick, in turn, has seen his role expand. He has become the vice president of player personnel.

"The situation has worked out perfectly," Dick admits.

"I enjoyed my time as color commentator, but I'm certain that Cotton will do a much better job. He's more colorful than me. I think I'm much more valuable in basketball operations than I was on television.

"Back in 1968 when the Knicks left me unprotected, all I could think was that there was no loyalty in professional basketball. My years here in Phoenix have completely changed that thinking. I gave and will give one hundred percent to this team and in return I have been rewarded with opportunities I never imagined would come around."

Dick's increased involvement in the front office has brought him back into contact with many of the people with whom he played. "Dick Van Arsdale continues to be someone you can always count on," observes Paul Westphal, who had played with Dick in the 70s and, more recently, has assumed the head coaching duties from Cotton Fitzsimmons. "When Dick played he was a fierce competitor. Every time he was on the floor you knew he was doing his best to see that the Suns won. I believe he brings those same traits to the front office. Dick has always provided this franchise with steadiness and class. I look forward to working with him."

While the timing of Dick's expanded role with the Suns moved him out of the deteriorating real estate market and into the Suns' front office, Tom was left to deal with Van Arsdale Properties Incorporated.

"Not long after Dick went back to the Suns, Butch left for a better opportunity in real estate sales," Tom explains. "In the end it was just me and a secretary. Without any new business coming through the door, there wasn't much to do except to manage our existing partnerships."

"That was indeed a difficult time for Tom," Kathy recalls. "He understood that the real estate market was going to be down for quite some time and he didn't know what else he might like to do. I could tell he was wrestling with the problem, but I didn't worry too much. I knew it would only be a matter of time before things worked out. Tom is not the type of person who lets a problem depress him---he's constantly searching for the answer to the problem and he usually finds it."

"I had some bad days," Tom admits, "but I knew something would come up. I tried to keep my eyes open for an opportunity and it was during this time that I was able to spend more time with my family and began to get involved with a few of the charities I now represent."

As it turned out, Tom's opportunity came from the son of his next-door neighbor. Eustis Paine, a venture capitalist who buys failing businesses and tries to make them profitable, discovered he had more interests than time to manage them and thus was looking for someone to help co-ordinate his various enterprises.

"I got a handshake deal," says Tom. "Eustis and I had always got along well and when we met to explore some opportunities we decided to give each other a hand. The name of the company is VP International. Eustis is the chairman, and I'm the vice president of operations.

"VP has is divided into three divisions---sports management, television, and publishing. The publishing division includes the magazines *Golf Illustrated* and *Fairways and Greens*. The television division produces a half-hour television program, "Golf in Paradise." Johnny Bench hosts the show, which features celebrities playing golf on some of the most exotic courses in the country. VP also provides professional athlete management services through Paradise Sports. Paradise Sports represents professional athletes in baseball, basketball, and football.

"Coordinating these businesses has been a tremendous

challenge as well as a learning experience. I enjoy my work and, more recently, real estate is on the rebound so it looks as though I've a future in that as well."

In addition to his work with Van Arsdale Properties and VP International, Tom has taken an interest in a variety of charitable and community-oriented organizations. "Food for the Hungry" is one such charitable organization. "Food for the Hungry" provides life-saving assistance---food, water, clothing, medicine, and shelter---to the world's poorer communities. FFH also devotes a portion of its resources to bringing long-term solutions to some of the problems encountered by these communities. The organization has funded projects such as well drilling, technical training and preventive health care, and has also funded reforestation and agricultural projects.

As a board member for "Food for the Hungry," Tom travelled to Bangladesh in March of 1992. "Witnessing the plight of the people there made me realize how lucky we are in America," says Tom. "We should not be ashamed of our good fortune, but each of us should be involved in something to help those who are less fortunate. If every American devoted just five hours each week to the charity of his or her choice, then many of the world's problems would be well on the way to being solved."

Tom has also started a program of his own design to help the parents of young athletes to deal with their children's involvement in athletics.

"I got the idea from being involved with Chris' little league basketball. Parents often have unrealistic expectations for their children. These expectations can cause the child to become resentful, which in turn often causes friction in other areas of family life. In an attempt to help parents deal with a sport-related relationship, I developed a seminar called `Super Star Parent.' It emphasizes the importance of unconditional love. I learned about unconditional love from my parents. No matter what Dick and I tried to do and no matter how well or poorly we did it, Mom and dad always gave us encouragement and support. We always knew that, succeed or fail, our parents still loved us. This is what I call a super star parent."

Dick, too, has done work for a variety of charities. "When we were kids, our mother used to tell us that when we grew up and lived in a community we should get involved in that community. `There's always a need for people to help,' she'd say. She's right. I've tried to do my part by committing time each year to a charity. I'm currently involved with the Epilepsy Foundation and I'm on the board of trustees of the Arizona Nature Conservancy. This organization is devoted to protecting wildlife in the State of Arizona.

"Within our community, Tom and I belong to the Thunderbirds, which annually sponsors the Phoenix Open. The proceeds from that event are devoted to charitable causes here in Phoenix."

* *

Perhaps one of the deepest sources of contentment in either twin's life has been their role as parents.

"Barb and I have really been blessed," Dick admits. "Jill and Jason have been such a source of pride for both of us. I'm especially proud of the way they've been able to make decisions in their own lives. They're both bright young people and we love spending time with them.

"So often you hear about parents struggling with their teenagers and there are many traps out there for kids to fall into. I suppose on the one hand we've been lucky, but on the other I think Jill and Jason are just great people."

It should come as no surprise that Tom carries the same opinion of his three children. "We have been blessed," he proudly exclaims. "Through my seminar, I've had an opportunity to deal with children and parents and I've seen situations that are not healthy for either the parent or the child. I thank God that Kathy, our children, and I are not in that situation.

"One of the things I'm most proud of as a parent is the fact that each one of my kids feels good about themselves. I once asked Chris to tell me if he could be anybody in the world who would he most like to be like. He thought about it for awhile and then told me that he didn't want to be like anybody else; he liked being Chris Van Arsdale. I thought that was wonderful.

"Of course, parenting hasn't always been fun. Over the years I've learned things about myself that I didn't always like and I've certainly made some mistakes."

Kerrie, Tom's oldest daughter, who will be graduating from the University of Arizona in 1992, remembers one such mistake. "I've seldom seen Dad angry or overly frustrated, but when I was young he completely lost his cool while trying to teach me how to ride a bicycle. It was one of those situations where he was eager to see me succeed and I was eager to please him, but I just couldn't get that silly bike to roll any more than several feet without falling off of it.

"At first Dad was patient, but by the twentieth attempt or so his patience had worn thin. Finally, he slammed his hand down on the seat and told me he was going into the house and when he came back out I'd better be riding the bike. I was in tears, but eventually did learn how to ride a bike. That was a rare situation for Dad. He is the most level-headed guy I know and as I grow older I realize how fortunate I've been to have such great parents.

"One of the things I've come to admire most in them is the way that they trusted me when I was growing up. When I was in high school many of my friends had strained relations with their parents. They often felt they had to lie to their moms and dads because they figured their parents would not understand the truth. My parents understood. I was able to talk to them about almost anything and I could always come home with a clean conscience.

"To give an example of what type of person my father is, when I started college my first set of grades were awful. Up until then I'd always been a good student, but I had not quite adjusted my study habits to the level required for my college courses. Mom and Dad have always been interested in my academic progress and I was worried about what they would think about those grades.

"When they got the bad news, they didn't say much. But within a week I received a letter from my Dad in which he wrote that if the grades I'd sent home represented my best effort, then he and mom were proud of me. The point of his letter was that they trusted me to manage my academic career. They were going to be satisfied as long as I was doing my best.

"Receiving that encouraging letter, when I'd half-expected one telling me that I'd better get on the ball or else, gave me a world of confidence. My grades have improved and I've come to appreciate my parents even more."

These same sentiments are echoed by Dick's oldest daughter, Jill, who is in her final year of college at Arizona State University. "If I've turned out well at all, it's because of Mom and Dad," She explains. "They have always encouraged me to be the best I can be. And they have always been there for me. When I look back at my childhood it is full of pleasant memories of my parents--- which is not to say that we never had our disagreements or that they never laid down the law with me. But they've always been even-handed and level-headed."

"I especially respect Dad for the way that he has managed to balance the different aspects of his life. Dad is a very busy person with a wide variety of responsibilities, yet he manages to give each aspect of his life the proper amount of time and energy. In this respect he has been a great example for me."

For Jason and his cousin Chris, living in the shadow of their famous fathers' basketball accomplishments has been made less difficult by the attitudes of their respective fathers.

"I know that every time I go to the arena and see his number hanging up there in the rafters I feel quite proud," explains Jason, who is in his second year of college at the University of Northern Arizona. "Dad has meant a lot to the Phoenix Suns and he's fairly well known. But just because he has been a high-profile figure here in Phoenix doesn't mean I look at him any differently than other guys look at their dads.

"One thing I've really appreciated about him is the fact that he never pushed me to be like him. I played basketball for several years and during that time I felt a lot of pressure to be like him from coaches and teammates, but never from dad. He would come out and shoot around with me, and he tried to teach me things about the game. But he's never asked me to be anything other than what I've wanted to be."

"The basketball thing has not been a problem for me at all," interjects Chris, who is in his final year of high school. "I never had the desire to get involved in it and dad has never pushed me or made me feel as though I ought to be involved. I play volleyball and when I was younger I played some little league, but that's not what I'm really all about. I just don't see myself ever making the same kind of commitment to any sport that my father made to basketball. I have different goals. I suppose the main thing is that by knowing that my dad had such a commitment and worked hard to be as good as he was, I realize that the same type of commitment and hard work will be necessary for me to get what I want in life.

"I learn from the example my dad sets, but I also consider him one of my best friends. Some of my more pleasant memories with him involve fishing and hiking trips. Dad has a deep appreciation for the outdoors and I'm glad that he has passed that appreciation on to me."

"I feel that way, too," Jason agrees. "My favorite times have been when dad and I go fishing or hiking. Over the years we've made trips to Montana and every time we go I learn a little more about nature and about my dad. He has a great attitude. He's always been content to let me be whatever I want to be and he's supported me in the decisions I've made for my life."

Tom's youngest daughter, Amy, who turned eleven in 1992, thinks her father is a great guy. "If he thinks I'm unhappy he always asks me what he can do to stop me from feeling blue. He tries to make jokes, too. Some are funny and others aren't that funny, but he tries. I think he's a good dad," she shyly admits.

* *

As the Van Arsdale twins approach their fiftieth birthdays, both seem to have found success after basketball.

"I don't really know what people mean when they say

you're successful or that you've found success," Tom offers when asked to assess his life. "I do know that I'm happy with my life, but I also realize that you don't stand still. With that in mind, I continue to look forward to the challenges of tomorrow. Its nice to look back and reminisce about all that has happened, but I still have my eyes on today's work and tomorrow's challenges."

"I'd like to think the best has yet to come," Dick responds to the same question. "I still expect myself to become better---better at my work and better in my relationships. I believe I can do more to make my life and the lives of everyone around me just a little more pleasant. My twenty-four years in basketball taught me many things about success, failure, discipline, and desire. In my years away from basketball, I've learned equally valuable lessons in other areas. As I look at my future, I try to keep in mind a quote I heard a few years ago. `You know you're getting old when you start having regrets instead of dreams.'"